Navigating Grace

Navigating Grace

A Solo Voyage of Survival and Redemption

JEFF JAY

Hazelden Publishing

Hazelden Publishing
Center City, Minnesota 55012
hazelden.org/bookstore

ISBN: 978-1-61649-616-6

Library of Congress Cataloging-in-Publication Data
is on file with the Library of Congress.

Editor's note
The names, details, and circumstances may have been changed to protect the privacy of those mentioned in this publication.

Alcoholics Anonymous, AA, and the Big Book are registered trademarks of Alcoholics Anonymous World Services, Inc.

19 18 17 16 15   1 2 3 4 5 6

Cover design: David Spohn
Interior design: Terri Kinne
Interior illustrations: Steven Gamburd
Developmental editor: Sid Farrar
Production editor: Heather Silsbee

Map of the Area of the Voyage

Map of the Offshore Voyage of Lifeboat

The Parts of a Sailboat

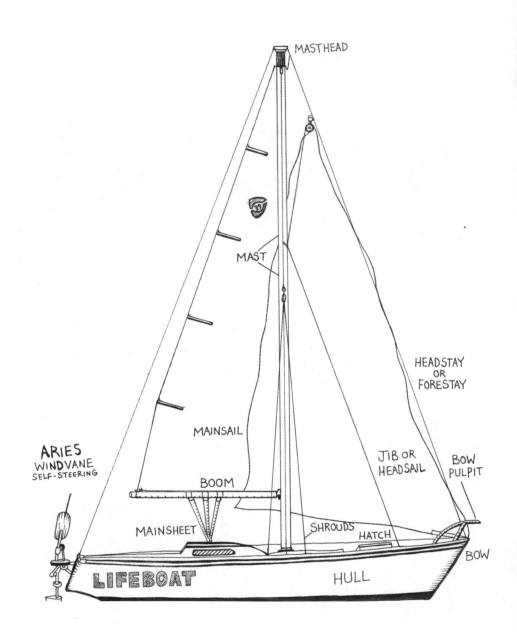

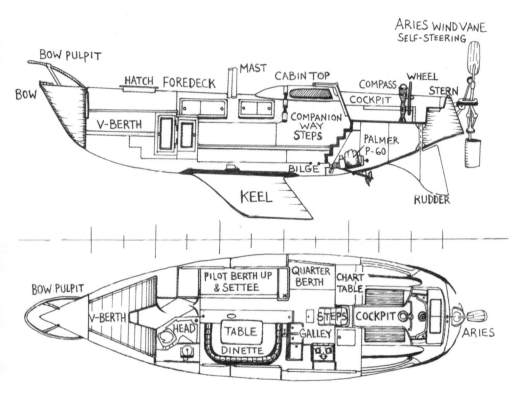

Contents

CHAPTER 1

Something Marvelous

"Just go," the young captain told me. It was an offhand remark to him but a benediction to me, a blessing on a decision I'd already made. There was no going back, but I wanted an experienced ocean sailor to assure me I wasn't crazy.

We were eating dinner in a quiet restaurant in Detroit, enclosed in a wooden booth that gave us the privacy of a confessional. The padded seats and heavy plates anchored us to the meal, and we engrossed ourselves in sailing talk, sticky barbecue ribs, and baked potatoes.

He was newly back from two years in the Virgin Islands, where he'd worked his way up from first mate to skipper of a good-sized yacht. I was getting ready to sail my boat to the same place all alone, so to me he was an expert, and this simple remark had instantly made him an oracle in my eyes. Truth be told, he was the first person to actually endorse my plan. All my friends thought I was nuts.

It was a cheerless night in late October, with the season's last leaves flying and the wind calling for winter. In the comfort of the booth, I quizzed my new friend about routes and rigging, ostensibly to get his opinions but also to prove I was knowledgeable enough for a 2,500-mile jaunt.

I had a big old boat and very little money to fix the innumerable problems that had driven its price down to rock bottom. But I had a vision of what I wanted to do and where I wanted to go, and I'd burned all my bridges behind me. I was determined to remake my life, to begin again with a sailboat as my home and blue water on the horizon. The young captain was polite, but he didn't quite share my enthusiasm.

Perhaps he knew what I didn't—that my dreams would fade in the light of day, replaced by the constant demands of an ocean voyage. In fact, it would only be a matter of weeks before I'd long for the simple luxuries of central heating, electricity, and running water. But on this night, all those problems lay waiting in an unseen future, like sharks building up an appetite.

The captain turned the conversation to his recent decision to return to Michigan. He talked about the consternation of his native friends in St. Thomas and how they'd tried to talk him out of leaving the Virgin Islands. Grad school was no reason to leave paradise and go back to the cold, they all agreed, sitting around the bar one night. They jeered in disbelief at the captain's descriptions of heavy parkas and ice.

"No way, mon!" they said.

The native islanders had only seen snow in videos, and they laughed and joked in melodic Caribbean voices about wearing boots and gloves. Finally, when the full import of winter struck one of the islanders, he craned his head over his beer and declared: "My God, mon, you gonna have to wear socks!"

That was the least of it, I thought. The young captain's reasons for returning to the States seemed pedestrian for a real sailor. He wanted to get back to his family, earn an MBA, find a good job and a good woman, and all the rest of it. I quickly steered the conversation away from this nonsense. If there were good reasons to abandon paradise, I wasn't ready to hear them.

I'd dreamt so long of a place where flip-flops hung loosely on sun-tanned feet and where time drifted off with the turtles. I'd never been to the Caribbean or even the Bahamas, but I'd read countless books and magazines, and I'd spent hours poring over details and laying my plans. I wanted to live in the calendar photos of pristine islands and quiet anchorages. I wanted to live my life out of a duffel bag on my own boat, skimming across the clear blue water, beyond the ordinary. I believed in miracles and knew Fate smiled on the one who risked everything. The sun would be that smile and the sea my promised land.

But time was running short in the autumn of 1990. The Erie Canal system, which leads from the Great Lakes to the Hudson River—the only feasible route to the Atlantic—would soon close for the winter. I was eager to go, but there were still lots of important shipboard jobs to finish. After I made it to salt water, the longest stretches would be offshore, at least 120 to 150 miles offshore, and I wouldn't be able to call for a mechanic.

I peppered the young captain with questions, foolishly proud of my encyclopedic knowledge. He was probably bored, as it was all commonplace to him, but he was enjoying the big dinner and he continued to answer tolerantly—though I felt there was something more on his mind. I was getting carried away with my own enthusiasm and the particulars of getting ready to go, when he stopped me cold to make a point.

"Look," he said, "you can't *get ready.*"

"What?" I asked.

"There's no such thing as *ready.* Boats always have jobs that need doing, and there's no end to it, ever," he said. "If you wait until you're ready, you'll never go."

He sounded just like me at my day job, talking to alcoholics and addicts as a counselor. Not being ready to change was a common excuse with patients, but it was a smoke screen. I was well acquainted with the myth of *being ready*, and now I saw my own delays for what they really were: fear.

He took a sip of coffee and continued. "You've got everything you need: a good boat, a little cash, and time. You can fix what breaks along the way."

I had good reasons for my unspoken fears, though. My boat was built to be sailed by a crew of three, at a minimum, and I had no idea how I'd manage it alone in the middle of the ocean. My self-steering mechanism wasn't installed yet, and I didn't even have the crucial part that attached its steering lines to the ship's wheel. My auxiliary engine was a hopeless wreck, the massive bolts that held the keel to the bottom of the boat were rusted out, and the list went on.

The captain took another sip of coffee and thought for a minute. Was he reading my mind? He shook his head and looked at me dead-on.

"But you're crazy if you go alone," he said.

So I went. And by the time I reached Annapolis a few weeks later, I realized that I was a little crazy, having burned through two-thirds of my cash before even reaching the ocean. I'd missed the weather window for the Erie Canal, so I had to spend a small fortune to have my boat lifted onto a massive semitruck and hauled overland to Chesapeake Bay. I couldn't wait any longer, and I was willing to pay any price to get the trip under way. My dream and I couldn't survive another winter in Michigan.

Two forces sent the pilgrims sailing across the Atlantic: the oppression of the old world and the promise of the new. In the same way, I was pushed and pulled by my heart. I had the dream before me and it thrilled my imagination. But I was also suffocated by grief and remorse. I had to escape, to start again, to run out into the sunlight and find another chance. Together, the two forces blended into one, like the push and pull of the wind as it flies around a sail.

When a stiff breeze meets the leading edge of a headsail, some of it passes behind, creating pressure, and some goes around the front side of the sail, creating a slight vacuum—like an airplane wing—which pulls the boat forward. And so a boat is pushed by the wind, as one would expect; but it's also drawn forward by the unexpected force of attraction.

So it was with me, both pushed and pulled into action. The dream of the Caribbean, a new business, and freedom pulled me forward with the strength of desire. But the second force came from the losses and a longing to escape, which pushed me from behind, out of the clutching past and into the future.

A lot had happened. My father had suffered from leukemia for seven years when the doctors decided he also needed open-heart surgery. He was dead six months later, struggling the last two weeks in an intensive care unit, unable to speak or even write. I learned so many horrible and beautiful things at the end as I held his hand. But I couldn't think of that now. I had to go.

Some years after dad's death, my little brother Greg, the one who was better and smarter than all of us, the star of the family who'd moved to San Diego, disappeared one day, sending out a seven-page suicide letter. He called each of us during the next two weeks, but wouldn't tell us where he'd gone or even what state he'd traveled to. He saw my mother just long enough to promise he wouldn't do it, and then he stole away and shot himself through the heart. And all of us with him. But I couldn't think of that now. I had to go.

My young marriage to a lovely woman broke up for reasons beyond all imagining. It was neither her fault nor mine, but I had to leave after I learned the real story. Sometimes the past can foreclose the future, with no option but to start again.

But I couldn't think of any of these things. There would be plenty of time on the boat when I could sort them out. If it took every last penny I had to get under way, so be it. There was a certain rough justice to it all, since I'd be at the bottom again, only this time sober. Nine years sober.

Dreams aren't born easily into this world. Like all the rest of us, they come screaming and blind, surviving only on the love of the dreamer. So a quiet part of me cradled the dream and my broken self and carried us through the hours. I knew my life with God was safe, even if this mad adventure killed me.

I had a growing allergy to everything commonplace, and I was determined to do something marvelous, something men only talk about and then regret not doing. I already knew what it took to sail all night in a storm, to navigate beyond sight of land, to live in the luxurious whisper of the wind. I was going to do something dangerous and daring and hopelessly romantic. Is there any other kind of dream? And though I was thirty-five at the time, I had the grandiosity of a teenager, the hilarious conviction of youth. What could go wrong?

The short answer is: anything mechanical or electrical. Old sailboats are filled with strange devices that are either rusted out, shorted out, or on the verge of giving out. So, one will start sailing on a lovely afternoon thinking everything is shipshape, only to find, at the most inconvenient moment, that a starter motor is dead, a pulley is frozen, or an indispensable gauge has gone haywire. Over time I became convinced that my old boat was the favorite haunt of little demons who flocked to its dark places by the caveload.

But I didn't know any of that as I sat in the cozy wooden booth, enjoying a fine dinner, calling for more coffee, and paying the bill. The advice of the young captain was the only thing I wanted to hear: "Just go."

CHAPTER 2

Invisible Forces

Sailing long distances single-handedly on a large boat would be something new, but I'd been sailing since I was a boy, and I loved it like nothing else. I longed to ride along the edge of the wind, away from the modern world and into the ancient realm. As a youngster, I'd been engrossed by poems like "The Rime of the Ancient Mariner," and I had an obsession with Masefield's "Sea Fever": "I must go down to the seas again, to the lonely sea and the sky, and all I ask is a tall ship and a star to steer her by . . ."

I remembered being about seven years old and sailing on Commodore Jensen's boat *Escape*, a salty boat with a light blue hull and brass winches. My dad and Fred Jensen were great friends, and it was an unexpected adventure to be initiated into their world. *Escape* lay deep in the sailing lagoon of the Detroit Yacht Club, far away from the gleaming motor yachts on the main docks. The lagoon was primitive and separated from the club grounds by a wall of trees and shrubs. Each boat had a wooden shanty tucked into the shrubbery, where the owner could keep coils of rope and spare parts, and the whole place smelled of hot sun on old wood and still water. To a daydreaming young boy, it was like going back to another era, another century, where special knowledge was required and danger was close at hand.

My father made a point of underlining the latter. When we were on the water and sailing a twelve-mile reach across Lake St. Clair, he explained how the sails were controlled by ropes called sheets and that they could hold thousands of pounds of pressure. The same for the halyards that ran up the mast to hold the sails aloft. These things had to be respected, he said, and told a story to illustrate the point. He'd been crewing on a large yacht on a race to Bermuda when a sheet had snapped with the sound of a gunshot and laid a man's arm wide open, nearly cutting it off. Sometimes, I could see, there were no second chances.

When the lesson was over, I ran up along the deck and hung my head over the side to watch the bow slice through the water. The world was framed by clouds and sun and wind, all magically translated by ancient means into sail power that sped us through the water. I loved the rhythmic motion of the boat through the crests, riding up and down, splitting the waves and throwing spray. The boat was heeled over athletically, and it came alive at the hands of the older men.

I explored the cabin down below too, with its primitive galley and cushioned settee, and I found a special place in the bow of the boat, where heaven lay. The forward cabin held a large V-berth, completely filled with sail bags, heaped up like old clouds made of canvas. They smelled like seaweed and distant times, like the ghosts of ancient mariners, working with their hemp ropes and marlinspikes. It was a dreamy place to take a nap, but I was mesmerized by the heeling of the boat, the pungent sailcloth, and the creak of the straining sheets above. I never slept a wink, but dreamed with eyes wide open.

Lying on the sail bags, hearing the water rush by the sides of the hull, I had unquestioning faith in my dad and Commodore Jensen. I was safe in their world, despite the dangers, and I stretched out on the canvas clouds and contemplated the tang of mustard on a good ham sandwich or, more importantly, the way the top of the mast danced among the clouds.

My mother and father had met while sailing, so the world of mainsails and cleats seemed part of my birthright. Standing on deck in the late afternoon, leaning against the mast and looking up its length to the bluebird sky, I imagined myself soaring off to far-flung lands. I marveled at the interconnection of the wire shrouds that anchored the mast to the deck and held it straight, the halyards that kept the sails aloft, and the invisible forces that whooshed us along.

Wasn't sunlight an invisible force too? It was invisible, but it made everything else visible. Wasn't that like God? I loved it all and wanted more—more sunlight, more air, more invisible forces.

As the day wound down and the sun set, we headed for home, leaving the distant reaches of the lake for the mouth of the Detroit River. After the sails were struck and the auxiliary engine was started, the men gave me the unexpected privilege of steering the boat, and not just for a minute or two, either. They showed me how to line up the frame of the bow pulpit with the landmark I was aiming for on shore. They let me feel the working of the waves, the strong current of the river, and how each played against the smooth sides of the hill, jostling the boat in unexpected ways. Their knowledge seemed limitless, and it was an honor to be allowed entrance to their world.

Years later, as a teenager, I raced sailboats with my dad, my uncle Randy, and my cousin Glen aboard a boat named *Sköl*, which was owned by Orv Aronson. By this time, I was a full apprentice, grinding winches and learning the ropes. It was just a Cal 30—a thirty-foot cruiser/racer—but we pushed it like a thoroughbred and flew the brightly colored spinnaker on downwind tacks. We placed well among our class and even had the occasional win.

The highlight of the summer was the Mackinac Race, a 290-mile sprint from Port Huron, Michigan, around Cove Island Light in Ontario, to the finish line at Mackinac Island. It was a full two days and two nights for our boat to finish the course, and it was often treacherous in the upper lake, when the big waves and wind threatened to sweep us overboard in the middle of the night. It was no pleasure cruise, but a balls-out run to a distant goal, calculated by chart and compass.

The race required two separate crews to manage the boat around the clock, four hours on and four hours off. Precision was expected and the nights could be cold and wet, but nothing brought me into the world of men like sailing. By the time I was eighteen, I was already getting in trouble with booze, but there was no drinking on the boat, period, so I was fully alive on the water. There was a special mystique to sailing night and day, a sense of voyaging and suspense. When the evening watch was over, I was grateful for a hot dinner at sunset, looking across the water at the kaleidoscope of colors. In the northern expanses of the lake on a cloudless night, the galaxy stretched out to every horizon and rotated through the hours like destiny's own timepiece. I had no idea what fortune might lie ahead for me, but I was eager to get there, and I wanted to hurry the stars along in their courses.

On my last Mackinac Race, we won our division, a miracle confirmed by the race committee. It was a moment of delirious joy for my cousin Glen and me, and we ran through town from the committee station back to the boat with the glorious news. Now we could hold our heads high in any company, but especially in the rowdy sailors' bars on the island.

Those bars didn't launch me into my career as an alcoholic, but after that summer, I went off to college and all hell broke loose. My descent was steeper and deeper than most, but that story will be told elsewhere. Suffice it to say the devil himself wouldn't have wanted me on watch, and in the end I nearly died. Those were difficult times, but through it all, I longed to be on deck again and lean into the steep heel of a boat under sail. I didn't believe there was a way back, but invisible forces brought me to a place where I could take the wheel and ride the wind again.

✳

In the first summer of my recovery, I got my old Sunfish back—the one I'd had as a kid—and sailed it like an ocean racer. A Sunfish isn't much more than an overgrown surfboard with a sail, but I sailed it hard and dared the bigger boats on Lake St. Clair. One day, I sailed two miles out to the shipping channel and jousted with the freighters. Then, like a fool, I sailed another ten miles up the lake, the sun burning my back to a crisp, and headed for a friend's house that was farther away still. I was obsessed with the dream of voyaging, but had nothing more than a toy.

I was moving into my late twenties and couldn't afford a real cruising boat, and I wasn't keen on racing anymore. I wanted to sail long distances, as long as the Mackinac Race, but without the rush. The first chance came to me through the good graces of Father Vaughan Quinn, a maverick alcoholic priest who ran Sacred Heart Rehabilitation Center. I hadn't been a patient there, as it mainly served hard-luck cases from the inner city, but I knew him from Detroit-area Twelve Step meetings. He laughed loudly, swore cheerfully, and challenged people to get off their butts and out of their ruts. I remember him driving the point home one night during a talk he was giving to a large crowd.

"The biggest pain that you and I have, that stops us from living, from laughing, from loving, is preoccupation with self. The anatomy of faith is this," he said. "Do the action first. Take a risk."

I was commuting an hour each way to a dreary desk job at the time, and I spent most of my days looking out a fourth-story window at the sailboats docked along the Black River in Port Huron. The smooth-hulled beauties called to me like an old flame, and I daydreamed of the time we'd get back together again.

One day Father Quinn phoned me at work, out of the blue. I'd never had a call from him before, and my eyes went wide as we talked. He told me he was going sailing the following day, and told me I could see the boat from my office window. Following his direction, I looked and saw the gleaming forty-two-footer standing proudly on the quay, just where he said it would be. He talked me into getting the day off and coming along for the ride. He said he was taking a group of patients out from Sacred Heart, landlubbers all, and he needed a couple guys who actually knew how to sail. I couldn't wait.

It was a bizarre collection of passengers that came aboard the next day, mainly patients who'd never stepped foot on a boat. I was happy to be a simple crewman on the foredeck while Quinn played captain. Another guy who was supposed to be an experienced sailor took the role of navigator, but with a bit too much swagger.

The patients were pretending to be sailors, tugging on lines and horsing around in the sun, all but forgetting the morass of their addictions. After lunch we had an impromptu Twelve Step meeting in the cockpit, and Father Quinn gave a little homily, ranging over some of his favorite topics. He talked about pain and forgiveness and laughter. In his rousing style, he raised hearts and eyebrows, and then he asked:

"Can other people see the unrepeatable beauty of God's creation in the twinkle of your eye?"

The question hung in the air like a challenge, and we all wondered if we really measured up.

"Well, you're the only one who can change that," he said. "You can't blame your misery on other people. Use your freedom wisely. You have to take responsibility for your own life."

It was like rocket fuel for recovery. Quinn wasn't a man to sit still, and his enthusiasm rubbed off on everyone. His perpetual motto was, "Say YES to life," and for him that meant *get up and go, find your dream, and give it all you've got.* It was a good day to be out of the office.

After the meeting, I moved up to the front of the boat and hung my head over the side like the old days. It was marvelous to be on the big water again, to slip the shore and get out into the timeless world. I stayed up on the bow much of the time, away from the chatter of the cockpit. The lake sparkled like heaven, and I was lulled by the motion of the boat into waking dreams.

Late in the afternoon, things got a little hairy. The navigator got confused, the electronics went dead, and the passengers started getting nervous. Quinn knew how to sail, but he wasn't sure what to do, and the navigator just wanted to turn back. I knew this would be a mistake, because there wasn't enough time to make it back to Port Huron by sundown, and darkness would send this ragtag crew into a minor panic. Quinn knew it too.

I took the paper chart of Lake Huron and plotted our position by dead reckoning, using the usual tools of the trade. I knew our relative course and the time we'd been sailing, so I was able to calculate our approximate position. We couldn't see the American shore anymore, and the Canadian shore was just barely visible off to the east. The question was: How far out were we? Lake Huron is over two hundred miles long. What was our best option for finding safe harbor?

"That's Kettle Point," I said, pointing to a faint bulge on the Ontario shore.

"No way," said the navigator. "There's no way we've come that far north. We have to turn back."

That was pure nonsense. The return trip would take at least six hours, and there wasn't that much daylight left. But the navigator was loud and insistent, and most of the crew were on his side.

"It's Kettle Point for sure," I said. "If we tack west, we can be back in Michigan in three hours."

Quinn was the captain of the boat and he had to make a decision. It was a tense moment in the cockpit, with everyone's eyes moving from the navigator to Quinn to me and back again. I showed him my calculations on the chart and we talked it over, and then Quinn gave the order to follow my course. We picked up speed on the beam reach, perpendicular to the wind, and made good time. The boat pulled into Port Sanilac three hours later, just after the sun slipped out of sight.

Quinn and I both knew things could've gone badly that night. As we were tying up the boat and getting things squared away, he looked at me across the deck, and I could see his blue eyes were serious.

"You handled that pretty well out there," he said.

I muttered some thanks under my breath.

"If you can keep your head when all about you are losing theirs," he said, quoting the Kipling poem.

I knew the unspoken ending, of course: "You'll be a man, my son."

It was a big compliment from a man I deeply admired, and I saw myself differently through his eyes, as though I were remembering something I'd forgotten or perhaps hadn't known. The following summer, he invited me on a major sailing trip with a group of better sailors, of which I was the youngest by more than ten years. We got into a couple of terrible storms, and I was proud to take the wheel on the graveyard shift.

For me, sailing was like a cloistered prayer, a sacred space, a dream of love. It was an escape from the clanging of the world, the hiss of electricity, and the prattle of motors. On the water, there were only the Zen sounds of the waves, the unpredictable moods of the wind, and the creaking sinews of the boat. Being far from shore presented an opening into solitude, and I wanted it badly. On a good old boat, teak benches were worn smooth as rosary beads, and braided line fit the hand just right.

With a crew of sailors, there was always the camaraderie of the sea, the loud laughter, and the perfunctory curses and gripes. It was a good world too, but nothing like the world of the solo sailor, who crewed his boat in the company of numinous spirits and the souls of those long gone. I was ready to dive deep into that world, to drink its magic all the way to the bottom and rise again. It took me quite a few years to launch the dream, but the time finally came when my old boat and I were headed for the ocean.

CHAPTER 3

Annapolis

I arrived in Annapolis just before Thanksgiving, on the heels of an early winter storm. I knew no one and no one knew me, and the sleet pecked at my face endlessly to drive the point home. The cobblestone sidewalks were capped with black ice, making me unsteady on my feet and uncertain which way to go. Most of the shops were closed for the season, and the restaurants that were still open were mostly beyond my budget, so I found a little market to buy bread and cheese and loaded up on carbs against the cold. Hot coffee and tea were my best friends, but the bottom of the cup always came too soon. The wind pierced me again and again, scolding me for lack of preparation and jeering at my dream.

The weather in Annapolis was eerily similar to the day I found my boat near the mouth of Lake Erie, only nine months earlier, and though I wouldn't admit it—even to myself—my misgivings had been just as strong then. I'd spent countless hours combing through brokerage listings and haunting marinas in Michigan and Ontario, trying to find a good boat. The search was mystical to me, because in this vessel my dream would take physical form. So I scoured the shorelines, looking through marine graveyards and down the marsh roads that might hold an abandoned treasure. Where would I find my dream or where would my dream find me?

A broker finally led me to a boat called *Relevé* —a reference to a ballet dancer rising to her toes. But this old girl was destitute, sitting in a steel cradle on dry land, surrounded by patchy snow. It was a good freshwater sailboat without serious damage, though she'd obviously been neglected.

But her sturdiness and deep-keeled seaworthiness appealed to me.

I christened her *Lifeboat*, and I had the name spelled out in huge red capital letters on the stern quarter of the hull, port and starboard, as though she really were some kind of rescue craft. My friends thought it was a death trap, so the name seemed incongruous to them. But *Lifeboat* was the vessel of my dreams, and charts could never plot the journey we'd take.

It was a Columbia 39, a white whale of a boat almost forty feet long, twenty years old, and cheap. It was built like a battleship, with seven feet of headroom in the cabin down belowdecks (which is called the salon or saloon on a sailboat), a large V-berth in the forward cabin, and a nice galley. It had a few notable defects in the way of equipment, but the Columbia was a thing of beauty, with a deep keel, sound rigging, and brass hardware. She had a flush deck, giving lots of room to manage the sails, and a long cockpit in the stern that ended in a T to accommodate the large wheel for steering.

I wanted the old boat badly from the start, even though it wasn't designed for single-handed sailing. This kind of cruiser/racer called for one person to steer, one to work the sails, and one to manage the lines. In fact, the two deckhands needed to work together much of the time, as none of the winches on the boat were self-tailing, so one person had to grind the winch with a big brass handle while the other kept the free end taut. For an overnight race, which needed two watches, six crew were required.

It took me the better part of a year to get her ready to go, working steadily through the spring, summer, and fall. During that time, I learned how to be a passable mechanic, a competent electrician, and a decent fiberglass and paint man. But when November came, I was still in the marina and the route to the ocean was closed, so I paid half my ready cash to a wily old trucker who promised to deliver *Lifeboat* in one piece to Annapolis, Maryland.

He explained how he planned to avoid the freeways, take secondary roads, drive at night, and otherwise elude the authorities, who would fine or tax the life out of him otherwise. Everything I owned was packed into that boat, and when he pulled out of the marina, my life in Michigan was officially over. I'd already sold my car, so I flew ahead to meet him, hoping he wouldn't roll the boat into a ditch along the way.

When the truck snorted and heaved its way into the Annapolis shipyard with the filthy *Lifeboat* on its back, a gentle afternoon snow was falling, reminding me that I was absurdly late for a pleasure sail to the Caribbean. Now was the time for boats to be put away for the winter, either stored on land in sturdy cradles or buttoned down in their watery berths and covered snug with canvas and tarps. Either way, turnbuckles needed to be greased and hatches dogged down before the owners and crews could get back to their fireplaces and dream of spring.

The yard was full of winterized sailboats standing silently, and I had a tough time scraping up a hand to help with the unloading, since all the men had been laid off for the winter. The guy I finally found was relaxing in a toolshed with a space heater and a radio. He met my request with a baffled expression: "You're launching your boat now?" Only my insistence got him to his feet, but, fortunately, he knew his job well, and the cold drove him to peak efficiency.

Hours of work followed, beginning with the delicate task of getting my nineteen-thousand-pound boat off the semi and into the water. A travel lift was wheeled into place, and *Lifeboat* was lifted from the truck and lowered into the brackish creek. We used a crane to put the mast back in place, then reattached the boom. The sun never showed its face; only strenuous work kept the cold at bay. It wasn't a day to inspire Caribbean dreams, and I felt a little foolish trying to make such a late start on the trip.

By the end of the afternoon, I was tired and hungry and a little overwhelmed by the job of putting the boat back together. Dusk brought a natural end to the day's work, and I was glad to head into town to find a cheap diner. But sitting alone in a half-empty restaurant didn't do much for my spirits, so I hit the local Twelve Step meeting and made some acquaintances. Isolation breeds depression, so it was good to get a break from myself. I was a newcomer at this meeting, despite my long sobriety, and the locals made me feel welcome, shook my hand, and steered me toward the coffee and cookies. It was good to laugh and settle in, as the people weren't really strangers, but distant members of my own tribe. One guy in particular would both help me and hurt me in the coming days.

When I woke up the next morning, my life in the Caribbean calendar photos seemed further away than ever. While I was in Michigan, the dream was always before me in the full color of fantasy, growing richer with every yearning. I could almost feel the warmth of the sun as I thumbed through the sailing magazines, memorizing the green-and-blue contours of the magical water. But in the time of that frozen Thanksgiving in Annapolis, I pitched the last of my magazines, like vacation photos of an old girlfriend. Dreamtime was over, the cost of the marina was draining my savings, and I still had a lot of work to do before I could shove off.

The next big job was getting the rigging tuned, a matter of art as well as science. My man at the yard put me in touch with an old salt at another marina who could do the job, so I cast off my lines and motored *Lifeboat* down the creek to meet the wizard. Disaster was soon at hand.

As I came to the first bend in the creek, I caught sight of a gorgeous yacht that put my old tub to shame. She was moored languorously along the bank, with gleaming mahogany and polished brass. I looked at her wistfully and was closing in for a better look when my old engine wheezed, gagged, and died. I sucked in a quick breath of surprise and terror. I was on a collision course with a million-dollar yacht and I couldn't steer. My ten-ton hulk was aimed at her bowsprit, promising untold thousands in damage.

I went into a panic of activity to restart the iron demon. I pumped the throttle, pulled the choke, and punched the starter button again and again. The yacht loomed closer and I wondered seriously if I could go to jail for malicious destruction. I just couldn't make the turn without power. Impact seemed inevitable and then, inexplicably, the engine came to life, and I got just enough forward momentum to regain control and squeak by the aft end of the big yacht, just inches away from her ample behind.

I wasn't so lucky at the marina. As it came into view, I could see I'd have to motor down a long, narrow canal and then make a sharp turn at the end. My plan was to putter in slowly, then reverse the engine to bring the boat to a near stop, and finally turn sharply to the left and gently bring her alongside the concrete seawall. My pulse quickened as I calculated the odds: maneuvering in close quarters wasn't my strength, and *Lifeboat's* racing propeller sometimes didn't work well in reverse.

I tried to look nonchalant at the wheel as the boat chugged down the canal, heading for the seawall. The crew from the marina were waiting for me to make my maneuvers, so they could tie up the boat and let the mast-tuner do his work.

"Slow down," the foreman called.

I acknowledged his warning with a cool nod, but I was extremely nervous about shifting into neutral or reverse, because that's when the engine was most likely to stall. If it died near the seawall, I'd plow headfirst into the concrete and destroy the front of the boat.

"Slow down!" he yelled.

Masking my dread with indifference, I pulled the shifter back calmly, praying for a smooth transition into reverse. The engine gagged and the men's eyes bulged noticeably. It coughed twice, followed by a sickening wheeze and—I held my breath—the damn thing quit. I feigned surprise and tried my restart routine, but nothing worked. I was so humiliated by the old tub, I wanted to jump out of the boat and swim for Michigan. The men started cursing at full volume, like a master class in blasphemy, and I joined in for good measure.

I pumped the throttle, goosed the choke, and pushed the starter button again and again, but nothing worked. The starter motor turned over, but the big engine wouldn't catch. I was doomed. As the men wailed and jumped aside, *Lifeboat* drove toward the seawall with ten tons of inertia, oblivious to the danger.

At the last second, I spun the wheel, hoping to deflect the blow so we wouldn't hit head-on, but the sound of fiberglass meeting concrete was sickening and the seawall was unmerciful. The worst damage was to my pride, which was considerable, but the boat survived. Thankfully, the business at hand refocused the attention of the men and me, and little was said, since I was paying the bill.

A modern mast is nothing but a hollow aluminum tube, and without the structural support of stays and shrouds, it will bend like a straw in anything above a ten-knot breeze and break before twenty. The tuning expert went to work on *Lifeboat* with a rare skill, so I wouldn't be dismasted at sea. He gingerly tightened the stays and shrouds all around, tightening each a little at a time, then going around again. In less than an hour, the mast was as solid as an old oak tree.

After I returned to my slip, I tried to adjust the carburetor, but its manual was written in a language beyond my grasp. Somehow I made a little progress, or convinced myself I had, because the old clunker started up smartly and idled properly. I didn't necessarily trust it though, even as I moved on to other tasks.

I had a hundred jobs to do, and my heart was failing at the thought of them all. If only I were sailing by Palm Beach, warming myself in the sun, halfway to the islands.

Late in the afternoon, a guy motored up in a skiff, wearing high rubber sailing boots and a foul-weather jacket. I recognized Tom from last night's Twelve Step meeting. I'd been standing by the coffeepot, blowing steam off my cup, when he introduced himself and welcomed me to his home group. I was glad for his amiable questions, and we quickly got below the surface.

He'd been sober for a few months, after two years of slips, and said he was still wobbly. At least he was honest about it. We were about the same age, so he was impressed that I was nine years clean and certified as a counselor. Tom had been sailing since he was a kid, and he had the look of a well-heeled yachtie, with neatly parted dark hair and expensive clothes worn with casual disregard. He queried me on my big boat and bigger plans, thinking I must be a trustafarian, but he politely curtailed his questions when he realized I didn't even have enough money to buy a good dinner. I knew what he was thinking and I was embarrassed.

Nevertheless, he volunteered to be my personal Annapolis tour guide and said he'd come by the boat to help. He knew I needed it.

Still, most of the next day had gone by before Tom showed up in his skiff. I had to swallow my aggravation, but I was also grateful to have a break. He nodded approvingly at *Lifeboat*, as though she were a good-looking woman, and tossed me a few encouraging words. He showed me where the crab boats came in nearby and what to pay for fresh catch. It was good to talk to someone outside my own skull. He promised to pick me up in his skiff for a meeting the following day.

The next morning broke cold with a smattering of sun, and Tom showed up on time, sidling up to *Lifeboat* with easy skill. I clambered over the side and we cruised around Annapolis, taking a tour of the town by water. It was nice to be a passenger and not have to worry about the engine, the shoaling waters, or the tides. I relaxed in a way I hadn't in months, unburdened of all responsibility.

When we arrived at the meeting, he introduced me to Dave, who was also a big-time sailor and also in his mid-thirties. It was a good meeting, and afterward Dave and I jumped into Tom's boat and we all cruised in the bright sun back to my marina. *Lifeboat* looked especially shabby when we pulled up, still dirty from the overland trip, but they looked past the grime and helped me with a few small chores.

I told them about my business plan for the journey and how I would use *Lifeboat* as a floating men's halfway house for chronic relapsers. I had an excellent referral source—a guy I hoped would send me patients once I got down south. I planned to make clients work hard on the boat, take them through the Twelve Steps of AA, and give them my own brand of high-octane counseling. The price would be competitive with any good halfway house, and two or three patients would fully pay my way. Tom and Dave said the plan sounded good, and Dave offered to ride along with me for a few days, to get a spiritual tune-up for his sobriety. I had my first paying passenger, albeit at a reduced rate.

On my last night in Annapolis, Tom and Dave came by in the skiff and whisked me over to Tom's house for a crab and lobster dinner. His small rented house was on a back bay, and I envied his furnace as I thawed out from the cold. The dinner was big enough for six men, and we stuffed ourselves royally over several hours. We laughed and talked like I used to do with my old friends back home, grousing about work and women and boats. The comfort of the evening's conversation made we wonder if I'd sacrificed too much for my dream.

Tom ran me back to my marina through the cold night air, navigating the shoals expertly in the dark. He didn't need to worry about wind or tide, as I did on a sailboat. He just pointed the skiff where he wanted to go and went. The stars shone like ice crystals, and I envied the cozy homes on land, with their running water and electricity. Was I a fool?

After he dropped me off, I settled into my damp bunk with tired thoughts. I remembered the old cliché: "Be careful what you pray for—you just might get it." But I shot back at the negative thoughts too. It was my dream and I was doing it. I was taking a risk and saying yes to life. Tomorrow I would be setting off, in any case, so I turned out the lights, shook off my misgivings, and thanked God for the chance to begin again. Dave was going to be a big help to me on the first leg down the Chesapeake Bay, as I didn't have the self-steering gear rigged up yet. It was a two-day sail, and Tom was going to join us when we docked for the night at Solomons Island, bringing the necessary charts for the south end of the bay, known in the old lingo as Hampton Roads.

Nautical charts were essential to sailing, just as much as road maps or a GPS was to a long car trip. One would never set out for a place in a distant city without directions, and this was even more important on a boat, when trying to navigate invisible reefs and channels.

The day before, I'd thought long and hard in the ship's store about buying charts for the southern end of the bay. I would only need them this one time, though, and the expense wasn't trivial. If Tom could bring the maps when we met at Solomons Island, it would save me a bundle. I had no reason to doubt him, but somehow it felt wrong to leave on a two-day sail without my own maps. I finally decided on protecting my slim wallet, but dawdled awhile in the store, looking at other expensive things

I couldn't afford. There's nothing like false economy to breed misfortune, but I whistled an optimistic tune in my heart and walked out of the store empty-handed.

CHAPTER 4

Chesapeake Bay

The day was blind with fog as we sailed away from the marina, and I continually had to dodge the lobster pot buoys that peppered the bay. These little devils were notorious for snagging props and necessitating underwater repairs. Dave had extensive knowledge of this part of the bay, so we made our course by eyeballing whatever landmarks we could see, watching the depth sounder to avoid grounding, and dead reckoning.

Other than being cold and accidentally straying into a restricted military area, we had a decent sail, but the wind piped up at the end of the day, and we had a wild ride into Solomons Island. *Lifeboat's* keel drew over six feet of water, so we needed to stay within the channel that led into the island's refuge. Most Chesapeake Bay sailboats have centerboards that can be raised and lowered, instead of fixed keels, so they can negotiate the often-shallow waters that can shoal up to nothing in the space of a few yards. It was touchy coming in after dark, but we made it and waited for our chart-bearing friend to arrive.

We were tied up in the appointed place, but Tom was nowhere to be seen. We warmed up some canned stew and looked down the wharf expectantly, but no Tom. He didn't answer his phone and he never showed up, leaving us both wondering if he were chasing a girl or a drink or both. How could he abandon us without charts?

Dave and I spent a cold night tied to an empty gas dock waiting for him to arrive. We then made the fateful decision to set out again before sunrise, chartless, and make a run for the southern end of the bay, relying solely on what we could reckon by sight. We both knew this was risky, but Dave said he knew the area well, and if we left early we'd have plenty of daylight to find our way in. We both knew better, but being men and not wanting to look overly cautious, we each put on a brave face and set sail at first light. We never saw the sunrise, exactly, as the weather deteriorated into a cold gray squall, which forced us to tack continually and make poor time.

By mid-afternoon, the rising wind forced me to reef the main, further slowing our progress. It was a long day on deck, and Dave was determined to do as little as possible, so I'd get used to managing the big boat alone. He condescended to steer while I reefed the main—a tough job for one man—and he scowled disapprovingly as I flaked the sail, calling for a neater fold. When night fell, so did the mercury, until it got down somewhere around forty. The wind hurled buckets of cold rain on me as I trimmed the sheets, and my hands went numb from exposure. Dave drank hot coffee and nodded approvingly. He ultimately conceded I might be ready for ocean work.

When night fell, we were nowhere near the entrance to the commercial and naval district, and we were already having trouble interpreting the flashing lights of the navigation buoys. The wind cackled with mad delight as a dozen channel markers came into view, flashing red, green, and white across the horizon, with no recognizable pattern. We were lost in the dark, and I cursed both Tom and Dave for our lack of charts, though it was solely my fault as captain. I'd known better from the start and that doubled the mistake.

Hampton Roads is a natural harbor area, ice-free year round, and home to the warships of the U.S. Navy, with countless shipyards and wharfs holding aircraft carriers, submarines, and massive vessels of every description. Norfolk, Virginia, and the surrounding area is also home to various military air stations, so the skies are continually sliced with jet contrails and thunder. The mouths of the James and Elizabeth Rivers open here as well, bringing a steady stream of commercial barge traffic, and on its easternmost reaches, the bay opens to the Atlantic at Cape Henry, bringing oceangoing ships from all parts of the world. It's no place for blind fools in a winter gale.

I take pride in being able to read buoys, navigation signals, and range lights in the dark, even in storm conditions. I've been fascinated by maps since I was a boy and spent hours in my mid-teens with full-size charts, parallel rulers, adjustable dividers, and a compass rose to determine the location of underwater shipwrecks. In my sixteenth summer, I successfully located a wreck near our cottage on Lake Huron that was miles away, purely by chart work and triangulation. It was like finding a pot of gold, and even though the wreck was little more than a debris field, the fact that I had found it—and I was confident that no one else had in many years—was a particular point of pride for a young navigator.

But on this night, I was utterly confused, unable to get my bearings, and openly worried about the numerous shoals and reefs. The channel we had to use was unforgiving, sloping steeply from fifty feet of depth to five feet in a boat length. The red and green buoy lights flashing in the storm made no sense against the background of the city lights, and they all seemed to be piled up on one another, stubbornly refusing to follow a pattern. If only a freighter or naval ship would lumber by, we could follow it in to safety. But I couldn't make out anything except the waves, which also didn't seem to know where they were going, heading this way and that and often slamming into each other like warring clans.

I decided the safest bet would be to start the engine, drop the sails, and motor through the obstacle course. It would be all but impossible to sail the gauntlet without grounding, so I brought the boat into the wind, pulled the choke, and pushed the starter button. My carburetor adjustments would pay off now, I thought, but all I heard from the bilge was a coughing fit. I'd waited too long to start fiddling with the engine, I realized, and dearly regretted my lack of planning. We were close to the first set of directional buoys, and so we were in immediate danger of running the boat up on a sandbar. I tried to crank the engine again, roaring out a string of obscenities, in case the Palmer P-60 was simply hard of hearing. It coughed sleepily in reply, still in dreamland, and snorted testily when I kept trying. It was no use.

There were two choices: I could either jibe the boat around and head back out into the relative safety of the bay, or I could try to tack my way through the maze of flashing lights. I knew from looking at a chart a few days ago in a ship's store that there were wicked shallows by the main channel. I also knew there were no safe havens for a deep-keeled boat as we took a starboard tack into the mess. I could try to make my way over to the naval yards, but I couldn't anchor there. The wind was mostly opposing us, too, making it harder to get to the safety of a lower Norfolk marina. The truth was, I didn't know where I was going or where I was going to anchor. I couldn't see anything, and Dave was proving to be useless. He was supposed to know the way, but didn't.

I tacked back and forth, edge to edge, running diagonally up to the brim of the channel and then tacking back madly at the last second in the opposite direction. I couldn't see the channel and the buoys were confusing, so I watched the depth sounder to find the edge. The numbers on the gauge would go from a comfortable depth of fifty feet to twenty feet to ten feet in a matter of seconds, and then I'd tack the boat on a dime and head for the other side. It was exhilarating and maddening, and I played chicken with the channel's edges, tacking back and forth for over an hour, finally coming to a decision point.

There was a small inlet just beyond Fort Monroe on the Hampton River, which could be accessed by rounding Old Point Comfort and pointing the bow toward a low bridge, but there was precious little depth for *Lifeboat*'s keel in the access channel. If only the damned engine would wake up, I could take the channel slowly and stay in the middle. Under sail, there was no room to tack, and the wind gods were toying with me like merciless drunks.

Meanwhile, my formerly blasé passenger was in a frenzy, hauling lines and grinding winches, and screaming that we were going to go aground and founder in the waves. His panic made me sharper, as though I'd been challenged to a duel with the storm. I'd been in much worse weather on the Great Lakes, and I'd just about had it with the whole damned night.

When we had a moment's grace, I gave Dave the wheel and ran down into the cabin. The molded steps that led down from the cockpit were also the engine hatch, and I lifted them out of the way and glared at the Palmer P-60. With no time for subtlety, I grabbed a can of quick-start fluid, soaked the air intake, and called for Dave to hit the starter button. It was like waving a bottle of whiskey in front of a sleeping alcoholic. The engine sprang to life, revved up to speed, choked, sputtered, and died. I howled with rage, sprayed the quick-start fluid again, and vaulted myself into the cockpit. The iron troll required coaxing and I couldn't leave it to a novice.

The Palmer responded best to a mixture of prayer and obscenities, with a touch of gas. I pulled the choke out to the golden mean, pushed the throttle forward a tad, prayed for a miracle, and touched the starter. The engine turned over, caught fire, gagged, caught again, and sputtered to life. I slowly eased the choke back in, nudged the throttle, and worked it up to a steady idle. We had power! The old motor even suffered itself to be moved into forward, giving us a chance against the storm.

We got the sails down unceremoniously and dropped them in heaps on the deck. Thirty minutes and a near-disaster later, we were safely anchored in calm water. The little creek wasn't meant for big boats, but it suited us just fine for the night, as long as the anchor held. We got everything shipshape by about 1 a.m. and were too tired to make hot food. It had been eighteen hours of hard sailing, and all we wanted to do was collapse into our respective berths. I wondered what the calendar photo of this damned day would look like.

A legion of anxious thoughts followed me into my sleeping bag and threatened my sleep. I was thankful for making a safe anchorage, knowing how many essentials we'd lacked. I hadn't even started the day with a specific destination—as though I could just tie up anywhere in a military harbor. If this night had taught me anything, it was that I was unprepared, foolhardy, and saved only by luck and quick-start fluid, if not outright providence. It was obvious I didn't know what I was doing, and if I had any sense at all, I would've been sleeping in my warm bed in my old house in Michigan.

But all that was gone now, especially the warmth. The house was sold, the job was quit, and I was a long way away from all my old friends. But I was doing it. There was salt water under my keel and soon I'd be rid of my passenger. Tomorrow I'd begin a long hike down the Intracoastal Waterway and through the Great Dismal Swamp Canal, and then jump into the Atlantic at Beaufort, North Carolina, for the real voyage. The only problem was that I'd have to rely on my engine for the next few days or be stranded. There was no comfort in that thought and no solution other than my prime directive: just go. For some reason, those words put a big grin on my face.

CHAPTER 5

The Boxer

It was thirty degrees out when we woke the next morning, with a clear sky and razor-sharp wind. We motored south across the bay, and I was mildly astonished to hear all the naval chatter on the ship-to-shore radio. A strong voice announced himself as the captain of a "United States ship of war," a statement that got my attention. He commented on the wind, which he said was "blowing right fresh." I wouldn't have thought a battleship would notice the wind until it was near hurricane strength, so I replied, "You got that right," but not on the radio.

Halfway across the bay, a huge object approached from behind, traveling very rapidly. What the hell was it? I turned around in the icy wind to have a look and finally realized it was a nuclear attack submarine, running on the surface and closing fast. We were motoring at *Lifeboat's* maximum speed, which was about five knots, while this 360-foot vessel was cruising in at twenty knots. You don't see this sort of thing on the Great Lakes, and I stared with my mouth open as the steel gray sub approached. Its massive and unearthly form raced past without more than a whisper, heading home after months at sea.

As we swung into the mouth of the Elizabeth River, the naval shipyards came into view on our left, looking as otherworldly as a space port in a sci-fi movie. Aircraft carriers towered high above us like iron mountains that somehow sailed the seas. A thousand feet long and as high as ten-story buildings, they stood side by side with battleships, destroyers, and support vessels—a steely armada come home to rest.

The long row of heavy metal was alive with activity, as men and machines tended to their needs. My sailboat was like a toothpick floating by on an old bar of soap, an insignificant piece of trash, unnoticed by the big brass. The power projected by these huge navy ships can only be appreciated in the flesh, as their size dwarfs normal human scale. Three fighter jets came screaming overhead, ripping the air to shreds and momentarily deafening us. It was hard to imagine owning all this stuff and not using it, but it was equally hard to imagine living without it, given the pitiless nature of the world.

We moved on. Our hot coffee had long gone cold as we looked for Portsmouth on our right and the promise of a civilian marina. Then a vision of loveliness passed by, like something out of a time long gone—a stately mahogany cruiser, perhaps sixty feet long, with gleaming white paint, varnished trim, and polished brass. It was piloted by an older husband-and-wife team from the heated comfort of their wheelhouse. Both were dressed in Irish wool sweaters, and they turned to wave as they motored by. Their white hair and weathered skin seemed like honors bestowed by time, and I knew they appreciated our suffering. How I envied their heated cabin, their steaming coffee, and their reliable engines.

The next leg of the journey would go from Norfolk and Portsmouth to the marshy countryside in the Intracoastal Waterway, so the engine had to function properly for hours on end. I couldn't risk a problem in the middle of nowhere, so a tune-up was in order. I pulled *Lifeboat* into a middle-brow marina in Portsmouth and paid for a night on the dock.

My money was low, and I was hoping I might get a referral soon for a real client, even if I wasn't in warm weather yet. My taciturn friend from Annapolis was paying me a small *per diem* for the ride, but he'd be jumping off the boat soon. As a certified counselor, I was hoping to land at least one monthly client, to help build up the cruising kitty. The clients wouldn't come on their own, of course, but I thought I had a surefire referral source in Jimmy C., one of Father Quinn's lieutenants at Sacred Heart.

Sacred Heart catered to the poor, the homeless, and a few wealthy dead-enders. The staff consisted of reformed alkies—from criminals to clergy—whose example spoke louder than any lecture. Father Quinn persuaded the archdiocese to give him an old building downtown, where he ran a thirty-day detox and stabilization program. Clients would then move to a converted seminary outside Memphis, Michigan, an hour away, where they stayed with us for another three months.

Miracles of hope were born on the volleyball court and in the cinder-block counseling offices, as the clients came to believe that change was possible. In the days before medical bureaucracy, the program was a simple blend of no-nonsense compassion and Twelve Step practicality. I'd been a counselor at the old seminary facility, and it was some of the best work I'd ever had.

Sprinkled among the clients were a few sons of privilege who'd barreled through more expensive treatment centers but never sobered up. *Lifeboat* would give them a different way back to reality, a floating halfway house where they could put their backs into running the boat, go to meetings in various ports, and gain confidence. But it wouldn't be easy to find these clients. My friend Jimmy was a sharp fundraiser and lobbyist, and he always had his finger on such cases. I knew he'd be able to steer a few my way.

Jimmy C. was born and bred in Detroit from coal-fired stock, a red-faced Irishman who could pick you up from the gutter or knock you out cold, as the situation warranted—a man you could trust. He was a pillar of the local recovering community when I washed up on those shores in the late fall of 1981, a man I was always glad to see, old enough to be my father, with red hair, powerful hands, sparkling blue eyes, and well-shined shoes. He'd come up from the morass of alcoholism to a position of respect at Father Quinn's right hand. He got donations, twisted arms, and politicked with the Irishmen who ran Detroit in the last of the good old days.

I first met Jimmy in Twelve Step meetings when I was newly clean, long before I became a counselor, and I liked to sit with him because he always had a positive take on the world. Detroit-area meetings are different than they are in most places in the world.

In most places, speaker meetings are common, where someone stands in the front of the room and gives an abbreviated version of their story and then invites discussion by a show of hands. There are also Big Book meetings, where members take a section or chapter of the AA textbook, *Alcoholics Anonymous*, and discuss it, and Step meetings, where a member will read one of the Twelve Steps, and people will take turns talking about how they worked that Step and its significance in their recovery. But in Southeast Michigan, we had an ancient pamphlet called "A Guide to the Twelve Steps" that we used as a jumping-off point for discussion among groups of eight or so people at individual tables. The guide dated from the 1940s in Akron, Ohio, and wasn't even a part of the approved literature. But this pamphlet had been the guide star for drunks in Detroit from time immemorial, and it lent a special flavor to the discussion.

When Jimmy led a table, he'd ask the same question any table leader would ask: "What Step would you like?" Then someone would request a Step, and we'd read from the pamphlet and talk about how we were working it and also about what was going on in our lives. The talk was surprisingly deep, and I was frequently amazed by what people shared.

I remember Jimmy leading an all-men's table and throwing out one of his usual chestnuts: "Gentlemen," he said, eyes twinkling as though he were going to wrestle each one of us to the ground. "Gentlemen, the attitude is gratitude."

To prove his point, he launched into a smoky story of hard luck, disaster, and reprieve. "I was a stubborn son of a gun," he allowed, enthralling us with a tale of early struggle, lucky breaks, success, booze, women, booze, catastrophe, more booze, degradation, and despair, with no hope of deliverance. Finally at the bottom, he spent a season in hell.

Then the tiniest shaft of light, too slight to grasp, cut through the fog: a detox bed, a chance, Father Quinn, and the ragtag staff at Sacred Heart. Over the weeks and months, he rose from the pit to become a survivor himself, delivered by grace, good humor, and a willingness to help the next soul who came into detox. He spoke with a special joy in his eye, ecstatic at his deliverance, like a sailor lifted from the sea by his mates.

At the same time, his gratitude came with a glad sense of indebtedness, which he was happy to repay at every meeting he attended. Although Catholic by birth and a believer in ejaculatory prayer, Jimmy saw God more clearly as a Group Of Drunks, who helped each other maintain the miracle on a daily basis. He was a walking testimonial. "It's a *we* program," he'd say, spreading his arms wide. "I couldn't have done it without all of you."

Mind you, we were all his juniors, and none of us had been around when he sobered up. But because we were all at the table together, and because we all carried our own pit of despair, Jimmy gave us standing when few others would. He thanked us for helping him, and we strained to understand the paradox, but felt its truth just the same.

To make his points, Jimmy would pound the table, point a stubby finger or throw his head back, and laugh a great straight-flush laugh, inspiring us all into agreement or at least a grin. His voice was hoarse from the outset, as though he'd been barking orders in a warehouse since dawn. He was frequently exhausted, running on coffee, juggling a hundred duties for Father Quinn, and hoping to somehow strike it rich again, which of course he never did.

Jimmy C. had a nose for trouble—not for making it, but for finding those who'd fallen and pulling them to safety. He had the determination of a plow horse and the wit of a country priest, with a ready supply of bromides: "By the inch it's a cinch, by the yard it's hard."

Jimmy would buy the best car he could afford, dress for the mayor's office, and try to catch you off guard. I never knew when he walked up to me if he was going to pull out a gun or deal me in on a practical joke, but all he ever wanted to do was shake my hand and give me a good word. "Just one day at a time, my boy," he'd say to me, "and easy does it." These words have a strange comfort coming from a guy who looked like a middleweight boxer—which, in fact, Jimmy had been when he was in the navy.

I remember going to a big meeting in the basement of St. John's Hospital in Detroit one Friday night. There were easily a hundred people talking and laughing as the meeting got under way, some sitting at tables, some milling around the coffee pots and cookies. The meeting always started with certain readings from Twelve Step literature followed by announcements. I ended up standing off on the side with Jimmy as someone started reading a lengthy piece. Jimmy and I had exchanged a few words earlier, and as we were standing there listening, I leaned over to him and said, "I've got three years today, but I don't think I'm going to announce it."

He turned to me quick as a blink, squinted his eyes, and cocked his arm as though he were going to punch me. I realized I needed to say something more, and quickly, but only managed to compound my sin by saying, "I don't want to call attention to what I've done."

Jimmy grabbed my arm, instantly cutting off the flow of blood. His quick move startled me, and my eyes bugged open. He leaned in close and spoke.

"What *you've* done?" he hissed. "What *you've* done!" Jimmy pierced me with stiletto blue eyes, glaring like an armed robber.

He released my arm and stood beside me once more, then leaned over, preaching to my flushed red ear. "You make your announcement," he said, "so we can see what *we've done*."

I turned to Jimmy to explain myself, but shut my mouth when I saw the old fireplug grinning. He nodded his understanding and gave me a wink in benediction. A few minutes later, I got the chance to announce my anniversary and Jimmy clapped the loudest. Since it was my big day, I was chosen to lead the table, and as much as I wanted to say something clever and original, the words just didn't come, so I mumbled something about gratitude. My old friend was sitting at the other end of the table, and he nodded like a patient teacher, glad to see another nitwit pass the test.

Jimmy was a fan of my halfway house plan for *Lifeboat* and told me he would try to send potential clients. I remember a dinner we had one night at a good restaurant where he deftly inflated my spirits, quashed my doubts, and encouraged me on my journey. Implicit in his blessing was a promise to populate my empty berths with patients, or at least that's how I interpreted it. I called him from Portsmouth, being sure he'd have a fresh mate ready for sailing, with a grateful family ready to pay my paltry fee.

Communication in those days required a pay phone, and I found one on a street corner near the harbor. By some miracle, I got Jimmy on the line and asked how my prospects were coming along. It was perhaps the only time I'd ever heard him sound sheepish, as he coughed and tried to put a good face on his regret. In fact, he'd made no promise to me about anything, but I knew he felt bad. He said he'd see what he could do, which was the thinnest gruel he could spoon out. I thanked him heartily, to mask my disappointment, and got off the phone. In those days, you had to feed the coin slot for every minute.

I was pretty upset with Jimmy as I walked out of the marina and down the warehouse road. I could tell he was never going to send me any clients, but I simultaneously denied it and made myself believe the story he'd told. There was no hope inside my belief though, just the hollow feeling of denial. I was off to see a mechanic with an empty wallet and an empty stomach, keeping company with the only one to blame.

CHAPTER 6

Mary Butler

Following directions from one of the guys at the marina, I walked a half mile to a marine engine repair shop that specialized in old iron. Traditional shops like this are the last refuge for mechanical relics—and human ones too, like the crusty old mechanic I met.

"Gas engines ain't for sailboats," he said, wiping his hands on a greasy red rag. "Dangerous as hell. Gas fumes settle in the bilge."

"I know," I said.

"I seen a forty-foot ketch blown to pieces," he said. "No warning."

"I've seen the pictures."

"You need a diesel," he said.

"I know," I said. "I don't have the money for a diesel."

"Well, the Palmer was a tractor engine, a Cub Cadet," he said. "Yours ever been rebuilt?"

"I don't know," I said. "The boat's twenty years old, but I've only had her about a year."

"How many hours on the Palmer?"

"There's no hour meter," I said.

"Jesus Christ," he said. "Follow me."

He led me to a room filled with old marine engines, sitting on the concrete floor like exhibits at the Henry Ford Museum. There must've been twenty different motors squatting there, freshly painted and smelling of new oil.

"There's a P-60 over here," he said, pointing to an outcast in the crowd.

It was primitive compared to some of the others, but I knew it was my salvation. It looked nothing like the rust bucket that sat in my bilge. I was smitten.

"I can sell you that engine complete for $750," he said. "She runs like a top."

"I wish I could afford it," I said.

"Son," he said, "you'll spend more just trying to get yours to run."

I knew he was right, and I knew he was giving me a rock-bottom price too.

"I just can't afford it," I said, looking down. "I don't have the money."

I could feel the old man looking at me. I studied the P-60 longingly.

What was I doing in an engine shop when I couldn't afford an engine? It was pathetic. He was offering me a perfect copy of my P-60, which would guarantee that my current transmission, throttle, and choke would fit and function perfectly, and I couldn't afford it.

"Oh, for Pete's sake," he said. "Where do you keep her?"

"I'm just traveling through on my way south," I said, with dim-witted enthusiasm. "Hoping to make the Caribbean before Christmas."

He looked at me cautiously, as one might examine a lunatic from a distance. Finally, he raised his eyebrows and asked, "Know how to adjust the carburetor?"

"Not really," I said.

"Oh, for crying out loud," he said and led me over to the parts counter. I didn't know what I needed in the way of needle valves and such, but he did. His directions were simple, and he told me to swap them out for the items that looked similar when I took the carb apart.

"Well, good luck," he said, knowing I needed more than I was likely to get.

The walk back to the boat was long and hot in the mid-afternoon sun and made worse by the heavy clothes I was wearing. How could the weather change so fast? I was humiliated by my ignorance and poverty, not to mention the puny sack of parts I was carrying like a lunch bag.

My boat and my dreams seemed too big, and in many ways I felt like a child who'd run away from home and couldn't find his way back. But when I got to the slip and started tinkering with the engine, it started up right away without me doing much of anything. I spun myself a quick tale about the cold weather stalling the engine, skipped the tune-up, and fixed myself something to eat. I had adequate maps for the next part of my journey, down the Intracoastal Waterway to Beaufort, and I studied the route.

Beaufort, North Carolina, was and is the favorite rendezvous point for Caribbean-bound sailboats on the East Coast. I was dying to get there. In Beaufort, which is pronounced "Bō-fort" (unlike Beaufort, South Carolina, which is pronounced "Byu-foot"), I would make final preparations and sail into the blue. I was growing more apprehensive about the ocean journey, but I shooed those thoughts away, hoping kinder notions would flow in right behind. There was a pretty sunset coming on, and as I approached Beaufort, I enjoyed watching the harbor lights as they started to paint the water.

I went for a walk after dark, spent a dollar or two on a snack, and shuffled around the marina looking at the other boats. They weren't old goats like mine. They sported self-tailing winches, furling jibs, and bright varnish. But Mr. Spit-and-Polish wasn't going anywhere, and I was. It took a serious income to keep a new boat in top condition, and high-paying jobs like those don't allow for long trips to the Caribbean.

I remembered the envy of the well-to-do yacht owners at my old marina when they found out I was headed for the islands. Their boats were bigger and better in a hundred ways, but they were busy with winterization projects while I was buying cruising guides to the Windward Islands. I remember a nice old guy sitting in the cockpit of his fifty-footer listening wistfully to my plans. "I hope to do that someday, when I retire," he said.

I was doing it now.

Much later that night, I was standing on the deck, leaning back against the shrouds, looking up into the Milky Way, musing on the universe. Here I lived in a tumble of stars, sharp and silent in the night, a thousand visible and a billion more I couldn't make out. My mind ran off to the scale of celestial objects. If the galaxy were shrunk down to the size of North America, the solar system would be the size of a coffee cup, and our brave little planet would be much smaller than a coffee ground, not even visible. And here I was, an infinitesimal being standing on a sailboat, thinking about it all. Thinking about Copernicus, Leibniz, and Einstein; thinking about planetary motion, orbits, gravity, and angular momentum.

The immensity of the galaxy seen through my eyes by way of photons that left their myriad sources tens, hundreds, or thousands of years ago, terminating on my retina, fed my wonder. I played with the light too, stopping it just a few inches from my eye by holding up my hand to block the way. Coming so far, yet so fragile, a quantum of light, humble and powerful enough to reveal distant worlds, or absorbed silently into my palm—traveling forever or transformed in an instant, but never dying. The conservation of energy, the first law of thermodynamics, eternal life for bosons—all these things were swimming in my little brain, housed in a vulnerable body swaying back on the foredeck.

Then, as I traced the outline of the constellation Andromeda and looked for the smudge of her galaxy, a shooting star tore the darkness, cutting the moment wide open. It was brilliant and bright with a long and graceful arc, lasting twice as long as most meteors. Its meaning was instantly clear to me, sending a shiver through my arms and neck.

"Mary Butler," I said aloud, as though swearing testimony to the universe. "Mary is dead."

The last time I'd seen her had been in the hospital in Detroit a few weeks earlier, and she had been close to death then. Though only a few years older than me, she'd been wracked by a particularly virulent form of multiple sclerosis, losing the use of one arm and both legs years before. Then she developed leukemia and lymphoma and God knows what else. When I visited Mary for the last time at the medical center, the nurse had ordered me to put on a mask, but I pulled it down as soon as I got to Mary's bedside, so we could see each other face to face. It was just the kind of defiance she relished.

"I'm not wearing this stupid thing," I said.

"Good for you," she croaked.

I'd never seen her so weak. She'd been hospitalized repeatedly over the years, but always made it back to her electric scooter, her sharp clothes, and the meetings she hosted in her apartment.

"What's it going to do, kill you?" I asked.

"It'll take more than that," she said.

"My germs would be scared to death of you," I said.

"You got that right, kiddo."

She was feisty, like a corpse cracking jokes on an adjustable bed. But I think she was relieved to talk openly about her death, which was now inevitable. We both knew she wasn't going to recuperate this time. It was a question of when, not if. Most visitors skirted the issue and asked perfunctory but absurd questions like "How are you?" Mary and I dispensed with all that. She'd seen me go through my father's death and my brother's suicide, and I'd seen her go through a gauntlet of torture at the hands of diseases and doctors.

"So, we're both getting ready for a big trip," I said.

"I'm a little worried about you," said Mary.

"Well, I'm not worried about you," I said. "You'll be trading in that tired old body for a new model."

"Amen."

She had to rest for a moment. The last two syllables had exhausted her, and she had to catch her breath. I wondered how much she weighed now. Eighty pounds? Sixty-five? There was almost nothing left.

"It's going to be great, you know," I said.

"I know," she said. "I'm not scared."

"It can't be worse than this."

"No kidding," she said. "I'm tired of being poked."

"You want me to poke one of them for you?"

"Ha!" she wheezed, too tired to laugh.

"I will, you know."

"I know," she said.

"I'm not going to see you again, Mary."

"I know," she said. "I'm about ready to go."

I reached out and took her good hand, which was cold and weak.

"The priest came yesterday," she said.

That got me, for some reason, and I skipped a beat.

"Last rights," she said. "It was nice, actually. I took communion."

That caused a deep resonance in me and I nodded my head.

"But I think I scared him," Mary said. "Just a young kid with a collar, fresh out of the seminary."

Mary had been a powerful influence in my life, beginning with the first year of my recovery. We were introduced by Ted Beebe, a flinty old bird who corralled me and my buddy Dick and hauled us down to a city hospital, where he promised we'd have the privilege of doing something useful. Ted was artfully applying an antidote to our youthful bluster, hoping to head off the self-destruction that plagues so many young people in recovery. He said he had a friend in the program he wanted us to meet, but I wasn't prepared for what I saw.

Mary had worked in the Detroit bureau of a national news magazine, and later as a speechwriter for local politicians. Just as she was headed for greatness in her thirties, an incurable illness kidnapped and dragged her down into a godforsaken place, never to escape. As if that could quash her spirit.

When we walked into the hospital room, I hoped we were in the wrong place, because this person was definitely not ready for visitors. Instead of seeing an attractive thirty-something in a newly made bed, there appeared to be the body of a child twisted under the sheets, emaciated and all but useless, with the head of a woman lying on the pillow. Was she alive?

"Hello, boys," she said, rolling her head toward us in greeting. "Come on in and stay awhile."

I couldn't speak and tried to cover the fact by pulling chairs up to the bed and taking a seat. But not too close.

"Help me sit up," she said. "This damn bed is killing me."

Dick and I almost gagged, but old Ted stood right up, so we did too, and tilted her torso up slightly, put another pillow behind her, and moved her into an almost-sitting position.

"That feels better," said Mary. "I'm glad you guys made it."

Mary sat at a sixty-degree angle on her pillows with a steel trapeze just above her and a hospital table over the bed, which held a single plastic cup of water with a straw sticking out of it. This cup, it turned out, was Mary's holy grail, and she didn't want any help getting to it, either. After we'd sat down and made small talk for a while, Mary pulled her withered arm out from under the blanket, grabbed the trapeze, and started to pull herself up a few inches, so she could get a sip of water.

We jumped to our feet to help her, but she waved us off with her eyes, insisting she would manage on her own. I remember watching her strain every sinew to get her head off the pillow, to get within reach, then struggle to wrap her lips around the straw and draw a cool sip. After taking one more, she dropped down onto the pillow and gasped with delight.

"Oh, that's good," she said. "I've been dying for a drink all afternoon."

I was in my late twenties at the time, all impatience and unappeased appetites. Yes, I was sober and working hard at my own recovery, writing music, and hungry for all things spiritual (as long as they weren't religious), but I was still in my twenties and filled with all the desires that captivate young men. But in that moment of Mary's struggle, watching the intense effort required to get a sip of water, all my fires were momentarily doused. I was devoted to Mary Butler in my small way from that moment forward.

We all laughed at her "dying for a drink" line and proceeded with our informal Twelve Step meeting. Most people roll their eyes at clichés and maxims, and I was no exception. But a few minutes later, when Mary started off her sharing with an old bromide, I thought Jesus, Krishna, and Buddha had flown down into her broken body and spoken the Truth of all ages:

"When life gives you lemons, make lemonade," she said.

Mary spoke about her gratitude for life, for God, and even for us—just because we came to visit. This last point made me feel small, as I'd been obsessed with my own little problems only moments before, with no greater vision. But Mary swept all that away with a bemused energy that belied her crippled body. You could see it in her eyes—the soft light, the secret laughter, the joy. I was drawn to the heaven in her eyes, drawn into her heart or perhaps into some greater heart.

I thought about Mary lying in bed alone all day, looking out at the sunshine she couldn't feel, inhabiting a ruined body that would never work again, catheterized, crippled, and thirsty. But in this moment, she was grateful—grateful for us, for me, for we. I could barely grasp what I was seeing and hearing, but I could feel the truth of it and I hung on every word.

"I have come to believe that miracles happen one millimeter at a time," she said, lying under the trapeze.

For years to come, I came to see Mary every Tuesday evening for an unlisted Twelve Step meeting in the living room of her condo. A handful of friends made the pilgrimage to her building in downtown Detroit. She spent hours preparing for these meetings, requiring help from a nurse's aide to get out of bed, bathe, and get dressed. Then more time to style her strawberry blonde hair and put on her makeup, until her appearance was flawless. She greeted each one of us at the door, perched on "Rosie," her electric tricycle scooter, her useless limbs strapped down for safety. She asked about our lives and loves in detail, cracked jokes, and sipped water through a straw—her blue eyes laughing, her good arm waving, and her spirit expanding over all of us.

I found open air every Tuesday night at Mary's, as I made my way through the thicket of those years. My difficulties shriveled in the presence of her suffering. She dismissed labels like "brave" and brushed off sympathy with a wave of her gimpy arm, throwing back her head to laugh every chance she got.

When I bellyached about nonsense, Mary listened quietly and then volleyed with one of her maxims. Cliché or no, when Mary said, "Wear your life like a loose garment," I exhaled and let myself go limp. Only Mary could say such things with authority.

So on that clear, cold night as I stood out on the foredeck of my sloop, looking up at the galaxy and naming the constellations, I was instantly covered with goose bumps by the sight of the shooting star, so much brighter than normal and traveling such a tremendous distance across the darkness. "Mary Butler," I said aloud. "Mary is dead." But I knew that she was more alive than ever, free of the prison and free of the pain. Mary was right there before my eyes, streaking across the night, not falling to earth like a meteor, but streaking off into eternity like God's own comet.

No, Mary wasn't dead, but off on a new adventure in the company of her peers, and I knew she would have a great ride. "Go for it!" I called out across the water, across the Milky Way, across the years. Perhaps she couldn't hear me any more than a sailor leaving harbor can hear the cry of a kid brother left on shore. But I called out just the same and waved, my heart so filled with joy.

CHAPTER 7

Gulf Stream Magic

"Stay out of the ocean," barked my uncle Randy. He was confined to a wheelchair in his home in St. Clair, Michigan, but still talked as if he'd kick my ass if I didn't follow his orders to the letter. Even in old age, with his health gone, he was a son of a bitch.

Uncle Randy (I never called him anything else) was one of my most important sailing instructors, and I'd come to visit him while I was preparing *Lifeboat* for the journey. I'd wanted to tell him about my trip to the Caribbean, my boat, and my plans, expecting that he would be at least satisfied by the depth of the keel. I should've known better.

Uncle Randy was cantankerous and angry to the bone, raised in Hattiesburg, Mississippi, schooled in the army, and disgusted by Yankees. He married my mother's oldest sister in the middle of World War II, and he commanded a brace of antiaircraft guns in Newfoundland. He was mildly successful in his small business, selling machinery to the automotive industry, and he lived with my sweet, sweet Aunt Mary and three kids about a mile from our home. In his younger years, he'd owned a handsome mahogany sailboat named *Yawl's Rebel*, which I'd only seen in pictures.

In my late teens, I apprenticed under him through two long seasons, learning the anatomy of sailing with military precision aboard *Sköl*. The owner was a kindly man who valued Randy's vast knowledge. The crew was rounded out by my cousin Glen, Randy's son, who was like a brother to me. We both worked the foredeck and cursed Randy under our breath.

We raced every Saturday, starting in late spring and finishing with the Bluenose race in the fall, slicing the waves in sun, wind, and squall. We learned the arts of sail trim and tactics, rounding the windward mark, raising the spinnaker, and running for the finish. We usually weren't the first over the line, as there were many larger and faster boats in our class, but we won our share on corrected time.

The big event of the year was the Mackinac Race, a venerable, long-distance slugfest. It was often stormy in northern Lake Huron, requiring lifelines at night to keep everyone on deck. Glen and I froze our fingers off as we changed headsails in the spray.

Randy was a hard-headed bigot with a frightening temper, but I respected his opinion on all things that concerned sailing. From him I learned how to use a radio direction finder on heaving seas in the dead of night. From him I learned the skills of a foredeck man, changing sails in the worst conditions, long before the era of roller-furling sails. We did things by hand, with brass hanks on steel stays, which made our hands even colder than they already were in the screaming wind. He taught a young man courage by throwing him out on deck in the dark and hollering orders over the gale. Uncle Randy just assumed you wouldn't do some dumb-ass thing like fall overboard. Though he wouldn't have been caught dead in a church, he enforced Ecclesiastes's maxim: "The fear of the Lord is the beginning of wisdom."

Glen and I took the brunt of Randy's tongue-lashings, being foolish and lackadaisical in the way of teenage boys. But we delighted in his swearing and irreverence, because it brought us into the unknown realm of military men. During the Mackinac Race, when Randy had to wake us for the 4 a.m. shift, he'd stick his bald head down the hatch and scream, "Drop your cocks and grab your socks!" We loved to hate him.

Randy had raced more than two decades trying for the Mackinac trophy, and we won our class in 1973. It was astonishing for a boat our size to win against larger boats, and Glen and I were thrilled with the win. Yet there was no celebration with Randy, and I never felt any special bond in winning it with him. None of us did.

So how was I supposed to stay out of the ocean? The statement was an insult wrapped in a direct order. What he was saying with those five little words was: "You don't know what the hell you're doing, you've never sailed single-handed in a boat that damn big, you have no saltwater experience, and you're a dumb-ass to even think you can do it."

I wanted to argue, but he was crippled and weak, and on many levels I knew he was right. I didn't care, of course, as I'd made my mind up to go. But his iron-willed directive, "Stay out of the ocean," rankled me badly and ultimately haunted me as few words ever had. I never revealed his warning to another soul.

⁂

In Beaufort I was alone with *Lifeboat*, moored off the old town wharf in Taylor Creek. The waterfront was lined with marine stores, restaurants, and galleries, but the main attraction was a surprisingly helpful library and maritime museum.

After a few days of fitting-out, I was almost ready, especially with the addition of my prized possession: an Aries wind vane self-steering mechanism, attached to the stern. I bought the ungainly device used from Hal Roth, the famous circumnavigator, before he set off on a round-the-world race from Newport, Rhode Island, six months earlier. This contraption would make single-handed ocean sailing possible, steering the boat true to the wind by an ingenious combination of pulleys, ropes, and gears.

The mechanism required no electricity, but rather harnessed the power of the moving water and wind, transferring it to the wheel to keep the boat on course. As it happened, I was missing the wheel drum, the last crucial part that made everything work, but I had neither the time nor the money to have one shipped. I jury-rigged an acceptable solution and tightened everything down as best I could. I should've given the mechanism a thorough sea trial, but it was getting colder every day, and I was impatient to get under way.

Just go, I thought. *If it breaks, I'll fix it.*

The boat had no heat when I was anchored out, so the cabin was only warming to about fifty-five degrees during the day, and it was cold as a tomb at night. I was sick of the constant chill and sick of my slow progress. I wanted to get into the calendar photo of the Caribbean so I could reheat my bones—if only it weren't a thousand miles away. I didn't want to admit how apprehensive I was, even to myself. Would the self-steering mechanism work? Would the old rigging hold up in a blow?

On the day I set out, the wind had dropped to a light breeze and the visibility was poor, with no chance of locating the sun in the sky. As I looked ahead over the deckhouse, a gray fog obscured the horizon, blanketing my uncertainty. I figured it would be a week or more before I would drop anchor again, making port in West Palm Beach for final provisioning. But on my first day, there was only cold and gray, with not so much as a single ray of sunshine. I headed straight into the fog.

Silence was a balm for me, and as I set the sails and killed the engine, I luxuriated in it. The thick salt air was dense with secrets, its hush only broken by a cresting wave or a groaning line. I stood with both hands on the wheel looking into the fog and checking my compass for direction. If my prime directive was "just go," I was now officially gone. After a time, I relaxed and sat up on the high side of the cockpit coaming, with one hand on the wheel. I felt no urge to fill the void, but simply listened as it sang its songs for me.

The LORAN, the electronic navigation device, displayed only numbers, so unless I wanted to calculate their meaning on a chart, the readout was meaningless. I kept a keen watch for coastal shipping traffic, as I knew it was all too easy to be surprised by a freighter coming out of the haze. I couldn't afford radar, and *Lifeboat* was probably too small to appear on a big ship's screen.

Sailboats are neither fast nor maneuverable, but there is even less maneuverability in an oceangoing freighter. I remembered reading about a huge container ship coming into a Pacific port some years earlier, after crossing the ocean. It had the mast of a good-sized sailboat snagged on its mammoth bow anchor. No one had any idea where or when the freighter had intercepted the godforsaken vessel, as nothing could be heard above the din of the massive engine, but the sailboat had been broken to bits, that was certain.

In the middle of the night, in the middle of a storm, many things can happen quickly with no recourse. One moment you're reaching along nicely through the fog, the next you spy the freighter on collision course and realize you can't avoid it and have to decide whether to abandon ship without provisions or hold on and hope for a miracle. "Stay with the ship," is the rule of thumb, but there's no guarantee. And no miracle had come for those sailors as the unknowing iron maiden had hooked their mast and crushed their hull. The inertial force of a nine-hundred-foot vessel, fully loaded with cargo and cruising at fifteen knots, would make their fiberglass hull seem like an eggshell under a truck tire. One can only hope they didn't suffer long, hanging from the great anchor's fluke.

I reckoned the visibility on that morning to be less than three hundred yards, more than enough to avoid a collision, as long as I saw the ship as soon as it came out of the mist. I was dressed in dirty-yellow foul-weather gear over a winter coat and several layers of clothing. Some hours and miles later, the coastal fog thinned out, and the sun started burning its way free of the clouds. I peeled off my jacket, glad to be free of a layer, though there would be no sun tanning that day.

By mid-afternoon, I'd made thirty-five nautical miles east-southeast, heading for the Gulf Stream. My plan was to get offshore about 120 to 150 miles east, past the main current of the Gulf Stream, then turn right and head for the Straits of Florida. I needed to get out that far to avoid the shipping traffic and the northward push of the current.

As the hours wore on, I immersed myself in the silence and simple chores of sailing. What might have been monotonous for others was relaxing for me, as the layers of shore life fell away. My ship was launched now, out on the face of the ocean. I was free of the endless preparations, the narrow channels, and the constraints of my wallet. Out here I had everything I needed: a strong boat, full provisions, and a moderate breeze. *Lifeboat* seemed to be headed outside of time, and I seemed to be a sailor from another age, a solitary soul gliding across the water. Just me and God, riding the swells. And a prankster.

I was lolling back at the wheel in an expansive reverie, when a loud noise pierced the silence just behind me. I jumped up, whirled around, and there, laughing at me from the water, was a grinning dolphin. These mammals aren't just smart; they're comedians with a wicked sense of humor. This particular dolphin had been clowning around near the boat with his brother for some time and then disappeared. Apparently, I wasn't giving them enough attention, because he snuck up right behind me, as close as he could get, and then barked. I jumped out of my skin, and he started cackling like a madman, laughing in my face before he ran away. I cussed him jovially and had a good laugh myself.

One of the great pleasures of long-distance sailing is to have a good hot meal at night. *Lifeboat* had an alcohol-fired stove mounted on gimbals to keep it level, no matter how far the boat was heeled over. I made coffee and a pot of beef stew, then brought it all up to the cockpit with two thick slices of bread. The steaming bowl of beef, potatoes, carrots, and onions was thick with sauce and calories. The Aries was working flawlessly, belying my fears and holding my tack straight and true. Looking up, I could see the sails were full and coursing through the sky like my personal flags of freedom. I was truly captain of my dream now, with a princely dinner and a good day done. Scooping up the stew with a piece of bread, I thought, "Farewell to you onshore," and saluted astern with the crust. It was a marvelous meal, and when I was finished, I put the metal pot and silverware in a mesh bag along with my plastic dish and threw the whole mess over the side on a line to wash. In ten minutes the kit was spotless.

As I moved into the warm waters of the Gulf Stream, the air temperature rose, so I took off my parka and enjoyed the mild night air. The clouds were still impenetrable as the breeze swung to the south, and I trimmed the sails accordingly. It was odd to have the night air so much warmer than the day—and in the month of December to boot. What a difference from Beaufort's damp cold and the loneliness of the anchorage.

Now I was really on my way, I thought, crossing a magic carpet of moving water, warm enough to toast the winter night. The darkness was absolute, with no lights anywhere but my own: red to port, green to starboard, and a white light off the stern. The compass glowed faithfully in the binnacle, which stood before the wheel.

My eyes adjusted to the darkness, and through the cracks in the clouds, a star winked at me on its journey through the galaxy—like a beautiful stranger making eye contact on a crowded city sidewalk, then lost in the rush of people. And how many ways was I moving at that instant? The boat was moving southeasterly across the water, but the Gulf Stream was flowing north like a conveyor belt, so I'd have to correct for current when I plotted my position on the chart.

I pictured the earth spinning on its axis, doing a pirouette with the moon, the pair dancing around the sun, and the sun itself drifting through the local neighborhood of stars. All these movements were mine, as well, and many more which couldn't be plotted on any chart. For now, the most important motion was *Lifeboat's* rhythmic loping through the waves, which I judged to be at about six miles per hour, the perfect speed for hope.

An errant wave caught me broadside, doing no harm but throwing a fresh spray across the cockpit. I looked down on the glowing binnacle and thought of all the tiny microbes swimming through each bead of water—tiny algae living in their own universe at the beginning of the food chain, converting sunlight into food and oxygen, which I now had the luxury to breathe.

And how many drops like that, below my keel, filled with life and multiplied to fill the ocean? The littlest plants, invisible to the unaided eye, are eaten by little animal plankton, still invisible, which then get eaten by things you can barely see, which then get eaten by some things you might recognize, like shrimp. Then the shrimp get eaten by herring, which then get eaten by tuna, which then get eaten by sharks. And a million variations on the theme, with whales and sea horses and lobsters and kelp, all invisible below the waves, thriving through epochs of time and surging into the present moment, wet and wriggling with life.

And now I saw myself sailing through the same epochs of time, accidentally atop the food chain—dependent on it, breathing its air, digesting its food, living its life. Seeing the compass through the miraculous evolution of my own retinas, having the ability to identify molecules by smell—my brain assigning them to salt, wood, and canvas. The incalculable richness of the mundane, lost to my conscious mind almost always, was alive to me now, in the swelling present.

What joy to feel it, if only a caress, if only like the star glimpsed in the clouds. What joy when the mind relaxes and allows its better half to reach out into the immediate beyond. Right here, the infinite universe reaching down to the finite human, echoing the laughter of God.

I never felt alone on the boat, not even for a moment. The balance of work and reading and daydreaming, leavened with food and sleep, completed my Divine Office, and when I needed a break, I took a grand leak over the side. I still made too many distractions for myself, but I was keenly aware of the companionship of souls and I tried to pay attention. I could feel the ages of humanity and the kinship of the ocean, and I felt it was a privilege to perceive it, however fleetingly, in the microbial hitch-hikers, the winking stars, and the memories of the dead.

I would get myself too busy with sails or checking my compass, but then eased myself back into quiet again, into the great pulsing energy of God. I could feel the world alive with power, beyond wind and waves, beyond gravity and light, beyond life and death. And riding that spirit like an ancient gull, I moved beyond life and death too, fully awakening from the dream and glimpsing the Eternal. But I couldn't bear to look that deep forever, any more than I could bear to look directly at the sun, so I turned back to navigation and sailing chores.

Around 10 p.m., I decided to check the sails and rigging up close and personal. I walked out on the foredeck and tested the halyards, neatened a coil of rope, and inspected the headstay. Everything was shipshape, and since the Aries was holding our course nicely in the breeze, I stood in the shrouds and hung my head over the side, out past the deck, so I could watch the white hull cut through the darkness of the ocean.

What? Something flashed in the water. Something big.

I jumped back, fearing a collision, but then hung my head out to look again. It didn't make sense. I saw a huge, iridescent tube-like thing streak through the water under the boat, perhaps twenty feet long and four feet around, like a sea serpent. It was clearly impossible, and since I'd only seen it out of the corner of my eye, and only for a second, I tried to chalk it up to imagination, though it clearly wasn't. I continued looking over the side, knowing such things weren't possible, when I saw it again. With both eyes.

"Jesus!" I said aloud, stepping back from the edge and grabbing a handhold on the mast. Whatever I'd seen was traveling much faster than the boat, coming from the stern, racing up to midships, and then crossing under the boat to the other side, racing to the bow and out of sight. It looked like a glow-in-the-dark sea monster, alive and swimming, charging past the boat and then disappearing.

I couldn't comprehend what I was seeing, when the apparition got stranger still. Could I have eaten some bad food? Was I hallucinating? As God is my witness, the exact same thing happened again, but this time on both sides of the boat simultaneously. From both port and starboard, two speeding tubes of light came up from behind, overtook the boat amidships, crossed in front of the keel, and flew past the bow in perfect symmetry. But this time, the serpents didn't disappear, but doubled back and kept crisscrossing the midships and bow, scampering around the keel under water.

I was watching all this with my mouth open, baffled and a little alarmed. I knew there couldn't be sea serpents under my boat, but what exactly was I seeing? What could be twenty feet long, faster than my sailboat, and glowing with light? Had my ruminations turned into delusions?

Then I got it. I was seeing the light trails of two dolphins playing under my boat. In the warm waters of the Gulf Stream, tiny creatures glow like fireflies when disturbed, creating a luminescent sparkle in the water. As the dolphins swam by at high speed, crossing and crisscrossing my path, they left behind tubular trails of light several times their length. The effect was spellbinding. It was bioluminescence on speed.

The wonder of the world doubled for me in that moment, as I watched these sentient beings put on a light show. Now looking for other signs of bioluminescence, I saw that breaking waves in my wake sparkled with light, and the little dinghy I was pulling behind the boat had a luminescent bow wave. It was like the Disney Technicolor shows of my childhood, with fairy dust living in the water, dashing here and there, and fading away before any of it could be captured.

The world was magic and I was alive in it, far offshore in the cradle of time. Was it a million years ago? Ten thousand years onward? My heart sang with the luminous dolphins and I scoffed cheerfully at their antics. The creator and the creations were indistinguishable in that moment, all of us laughing.

Was the wind picking up? The warmth of the Gulf Stream air seduced me. It had been quite a long day by now, and it was important for me to get some rest. I believe I got about an hour.

CHAPTER 8

Losing Control

I was sleeping deeply in my bunk when a terrible crash woke me, and adrenaline shot through my veins. The boat was getting knocked over violently, and I raced up the companionway to unspeakable chaos. I was looking at a nightmare and didn't know what to do first.

The Aries self-steering mechanism had popped off the wheel, sending the boat into a sharp turn, overpowering the sails, and pulling the deck into the water. The boat was heeled over at such an angle I had to climb the cockpit like a roofer on wet shingles. I made my way to the wheel, untied the tangled steering lines, and tried to get control of the boat.

Nothing worked right. The sails were backwinded, and they were pushing the boat over on its ear. Once I got my bearings, I was able to avoid the immediate problem of a capsize, but the boat was still psycho. The wind had really piped up too, so the rig was badly overloaded.

Lifeboat was on the wrong tack, so the sails were pulling the boat over instead of pushing it forward. I had to do something different. I tried to ease the mainsail, but this caused the boat to immediately round up into the wind and crash onto a different tack. As much as I tried to fight it, *Lifeboat* changed tacks uncontrollably in the high wind. The forces were so great, the lines attached to the cabin nearly cracked the top off.

I needed to be grinding the winches, controlling the wheel, and changing the sails all at once, and I was furious with impossibility of single-handing in this situation. I uncleated the foresail and let it flap in the wind and did the same with the mainsail. Now what? I had to get back on course, but I had zero forward momentum, sitting crosswise to the wind in the darkness.

Over the next hour, I somehow got everything shipshape and working properly. Without getting into a lot of mechanics, the problem was my makeshift wheel hub for the Aries. Basically, there was a line coming to the wheel from each side, and they wrapped around the hub and steered the boat. One line came from the starboard side and wrapped around the hub, and one came from the port side and wrapped in the opposite direction. Depending on the action of the Aries, these lines turned the wheel one way or another. A proper wheel hub would've taken two wraps of line from each side, giving a secure purchase. My jury-rigged hub only had space for a half-turn for each line. Clearly, this wasn't enough, and the higher winds made everything more difficult.

An hour later, I got back on course, and, when everything was satisfactory, I sat in the cockpit exhausted. It had been a full-blown nightmare, but I was satisfied with my work. I hadn't had any real sleep since the night before and was beat. Just as I was about to head down below, the steering lines popped off the hub again, setting off the same nightmare scenario.

The boat tacked uncontrollably, the sails backwinded, and I went into a fury. I couldn't believe the level of unmanageability. At the top of my lungs I damned the Aries, and I would've torn it off the back of the boat and thrown the whole contraption overboard if I hadn't needed it so badly. The Aries had to work, it just had to, or I'd be left to drift whenever I needed sleep, which would mean riding the Gulf Stream north, in the opposite direction I needed to travel.

Sleep was impossible that night, as my makeshift hub kept failing. The great tension on the steering lines kept defeating my jury-rig, sending the boat into a tailspin. *Lifeboat* staggered under the weight of my mistakes, and I was incapable of keeping her on a steady course. I was ashamed of my untried system and afraid of the price I might pay. Rain nagged me on and off through the night, just to rub it in.

I couldn't stay awake twenty-four hours a day. I experimented with one thing and another, always sure I'd found the cure. I led the steering lines from different angles, moved the blocks here and there. I tied and retied the lines around the wheel, ever so tightly, only to have the whole mess break loose again.

I thought I was going to lose my mind—or perhaps I already had. The nightmare replayed itself again and again, driving me to the edge of despair. But there was no one else to work the lines or steer the boat, so I had to keep going. I was too tired to think straight, and the rain continued to fall, first softly and then with intent. Finally, I gave up on the Aries and took the wheel myself, steering by the dim light of the compass, with no bearing in sight.

After a while, an old memory crossed my mind, triggering a chuckle that sounded more like a cough. Maybe it wasn't funny like a joke, maybe it wasn't a story that could be told at a party, but it was funny to me.

"This is nothing!" I shouted across the water. "Nothing!"

And compared to my drinking days, it wasn't. I coughed a little more and felt good deep down in a stubborn, satisfied kind of way. I'd escaped with my life at the last possible moment nine years ago, and the memory of my deliverance helped me steer until dawn.

Most people can drink socially, but some people have problems with alcohol and a few are just plain drunks. I was a chronic alcoholic by the time I was nineteen, and I had a knack for self-destruction that amazed everyone who knew me. Even my cocaine dealer told me I had a drinking problem.

Things weren't out of hand until the end of my first year of college, when wholesale insanity took hold. I remember lying flat on my back, looking up at the underside of a coffee table at 4 a.m., and thinking, "I really should've tried to get some sleep tonight, considering that the biggest opportunity of my life is coming up in three hours." But I arose from the carpet not to shower or shave, but to continue the party with the dealer and his girlfriend.

One of the faculty had arranged for me to meet an influential professor at another college and had volunteered to drive me five hours for the interview. I showed up filthy and drunk at 7 a.m., climbed in his car, and made an ass of myself all day. It was the first time my alcoholism had caused me to humiliate not just myself, but people I held in high regard. Neither man ever had anything to do with me again.

I didn't try to stop drinking, but I was genuinely surprised by how much worse it got. To begin with, I couldn't finish college, though I returned from time to time to try. I rationalized this by saying I was too busy with creative projects to fool with academics, that I was going off to look for America, or some other hogwash. I hitchhiked around the country, lugging a massive copy of Heidegger's *Being and Time* along with some popular stuff, like Kerouac's *The Dharma Bums*, to feed my rationalizations. I believed I was destined to write a great novel, but I didn't have the discipline to keep a diary, much less revise sentences. I was a fraud.

Then there was the toll on my family, my poor parents in particular, who did everything they could to keep their firstborn on track. I crashed cars, wasted tuition, and bummed around the country—north, south, east, and west. I told my parents stories (that I mostly believed) about how I was going back to college, again, how I was going to find a job, again, or how I was going to, I don't know, do something constructive. But all I did every day was drink alcohol, smoke pot, take random drugs, and otherwise submerge my brain in a chemical soup until I blacked out or passed out.

I frequently disappeared for weeks, and even when I announced where I was going (Atlanta or Chicago or somewhere in California), I didn't call or write for months. I couldn't imagine what I was putting people through, but it was awful and thoughtless and, in many ways, sociopathic. But an old-fashioned expression, which I would've dismissed with a laugh, would've been more accurate: I was sinful. And I was so in love with the darkness that I swore it was light.

During that period, I dismissed God and all religion, and I was gloriously, prodigally, mindlessly sinful, feeding every appetite until my stamina or consciousness failed. I was determined to have an excess of everything, and too bad for the tender feelings of family, friends, or anyone who might be foolish enough to care. I was on the road.

My relationships with women were dismal. The sordid messes and broken promises, the blackouts, the crashed cars and trashed apartments—it was all too despicable for words, and since I couldn't make sense of the problem, I doubled up on the solution: alcohol. Any and all other substances were also welcome, but alcohol was my mainstay. When added in large enough quantities, the brain fire subsided and the miserable day came to a close. All problems were solved.

Every year was worse than the last, every catastrophe more humiliating. Near the end, I surfaced and seemed to make a new start. I had a wonderful girlfriend, and I got a good job as a writer for an impressive business in downtown Chicago. I worked for the owner, drafting reports and other documents at a frenetic pace, often several thousand words per day. But by lunchtime I was in the bar around the corner, getting down to business. I drank for fifty minutes every day, starting at 1 p.m. (six beers and two shots), talking to no one and having no food to buffer the flow. By the time I returned to the office, I was quite soggy, but usually able to weather the afternoon.

Before long, I couldn't make it to work without a drink. I'd stop at an old men's bar when the doors opened at 7 a.m., rationalizing that I'd just have a quickie before getting on the 'L' (the Chicago elevated train). By 10:30, I'd be calling the office for the third time, promising to appear shortly. I made the situation worse by taking home confidential documents, which shouldn't have been removed from the office. I was trying to make up for falling behind, but I only got in more trouble. I was reprimanded forcefully by the vice president, but not fired, as the boss still believed in me.

He invited me out to his lakeshore home, so we could work together and get through the mess. He really wanted to help me out of my problems. I was scheduled to take a train out to his northern suburb first thing in the morning, and I promised I'd be at his home no later than 9:30 a.m. I took the 'L' downtown, passing by my usual bar, and made it downtown without incident. Now I only had to walk the few blocks to Union Station and catch a train to his town. Unfortunately, there was a bar between the 'L' and the station, and its siren song called me in for a quickie. I don't know what happened, but two hours later I called and told my boss some pathetic and transparent lie. In any case, I didn't get to his home until one in the afternoon.

It was a fine day, and I arrived with false enthusiasm, ready to buckle down and work. I could pound out five thousand words by dinner if I had to and make up for my tardiness. I rang the bell hopefully, but he opened the door as if to rid himself of a traveling salesman. He didn't say hello and he didn't say my name; he just looked at me impassively and said, "I don't need you." Before I could reply, he shut the great wooden door in my face.

I stood there on the porch for a moment, stunned. There was no recourse, no chance to ring the bell again and talk my way out of it. My great writing job was over, not six months after it had begun. I felt like I'd just been in a car crash, realizing too late that it might've been avoided. It was the same mistake I'd made so many times before in so many other places. I was sick of the predictability of my failures, always powered by the same fuel. No matter how promising the opportunity, I'd just add alcohol and the dream would dissolve.

Standing there on the boss's front porch, looking at the slammed door, I could feel the mixture of whiskey and beer in my stomach beginning to boil. I hadn't had anything to eat all day and had spent all my money, so I was really counting on a free lunch and a chance to borrow train fare home. Walking back to the station in the broiling sun, past the manicured suburban lawns, I resolutely thought of nothing except how I'd scrounge up some money for the train. I refused to think about how I'd explain it to my girlfriend, again, or how I'd explain it to my parents, again, or how I'd explain it to my friends, again. I told myself I was going to be a great writer, but all I did was drink. Stories and plays were begun, but I didn't have a fraction of the discipline required to do the work.

Amazingly enough, it never occurred to me that I was an alcoholic, though several friends and family members had used the word. I usually made some asinine reply, like, "In that case, I must need a drink," and went directly to the bottle. I preferred a brand of whiskey called Wild Turkey, because it came in a 100-proof variety. I'd combine a bottle of whiskey with a case of beer and have a fine evening, smoking pot, doing shots, and guzzling from longneck bottles.

So the Aries's repeated failures seemed familiar, even human. Fix it and it breaks, fix it and it breaks. Just like an alcoholic trying to sober up without a program. Clearly the boat needed a better fix, but I didn't have the right mechanism, and I couldn't manufacture one in the middle of the ocean. As the rain continued hour after hour, the water had a positive effect on the lines. Once the cords got fully soaked, they stretched out to their limit, getting slimmer in the process. When they were fully stretched, I was able to wrap them around the hub a bit further, getting a better grip.

The end of my drinking was similar, in some ways. Where rain had stretched the steering lines to the point of being workable, alcohol stretched and strained and drained me to the point of surrender.

CHAPTER 9

Dr. Keating

Hitting bottom has always been a lousy recipe for recovery, because a lot of addicts don't bounce. They just die. Others hit bottom and bounce along for years, because they have a good enabling system, or they go nuts or get locked up. But I had a classic bottom, an unexpected intervention, and an inexplicable deliverance.

After I lost the writing job, I had to sell everything I owned piecemeal to get by, drinking steadily through each day, waiting for I don't know what. My girlfriend moved back East, unable to comprehend my illness. An old friend, Mark Domin, and his wife, Diana, came to visit me in my nearly empty apartment for the weekend. They went to a Cubs game while I sat in the apartment and drank. I have little memory of their visit, but Mark later said he'd cried on the long ride home, because he was certain he'd never see me alive again. I was oblivious.

Soon after their visit, I lost the apartment, scrounged up the last of my money, and bought a train ticket to San Francisco. I made my way to the North Beach area, famous for Beat poets and itinerant drunks like me. At the age of twenty-six, I had a bleeding ulcer and a bleeding colon that weakened me terribly. I had trouble walking, probably from some transient neuropathy, and often had to stop in the middle of the sidewalk to regain the use of my legs. I couldn't tolerate solid food, I couldn't hold a job, and I was broke. I'd planned a brilliant comeback, but I couldn't manage to do more than panhandle money for a flophouse room costing seven dollars a night. I was grateful to have a little space to call my own.

I'd come to San Francisco several times over the last six years because it was the coolest place on earth. From City Lights bookstore to Haight-Ashbury to the Beach Chalet, it was paradise with lousy weather, and I loved it dearly. Since I'm unapologetically sentimental, I was drawn to the views, the languages, the shops, and the vibe. In San Francisco, like no other town I know, the air down by the piers actually smells like adventure, like white caps and old rope.

I loved to walk beyond Fisherman's Wharf to the warehouses where the commercial boats came in, with seals barking for scraps from the water below. Or out past the Dolphin Club on the great pier that sweeps out into the bay, like a backward question mark. Sitting at the end of that pier, watching the Chinese fishermen cast their lines, I waited for the slightest chance of sun, hoping my luck would turn. In those days, a gallon of red wine could be bought for $2.50 at the local supermarket, and a pack of cigarettes cost less than a buck. For a few more pennies, I could add a baguette, which would last most of the day. I was the king of skid row.

But at the end, I didn't have the strength to walk on the wharves or out on the pier. I barely had the strength to walk up Columbus Avenue to Coit Liquor to buy a half pint, so I settled for the chilly grass in Washington Square Park, a one-block oasis of green in the middle of North Beach. Here I'd drink and worry or scheme. I'd lost track of hours and days, and nothing seemed to pan out. My few friends knew they could find me in the park, and some tried to talk me into getting help, but I couldn't grasp what they were trying to tell me.

I remember an old girlfriend coming to visit me at ten in the morning as I sat in the grass with a brown paper bag, drinking my breakfast. She looked beautiful and hip, and she talked earnestly about my drinking problem. She wanted nothing to do with me in the old way, but she encouraged me to get up and do something, anything, but drink myself to death. I remember her sadness and frustration in trying to reach me through the bulwark of my cynicism.

Somehow I heard through the grapevine that Rickie, an old high school friend of mine, had committed suicide. He'd done it in a quiet and fastidious way: taking a handful of Valium and then pulling a large plastic trash bag over his head and cinching it around his neck with heavy-duty rubber bands. He laid down on his bed, passed out, and eventually suffocated. No muss, no fuss.

So deep was my emotional paralysis, so craven my thinking, that when I heard about Rickie's suicide, my immediate reaction was "Far out!" and I silently resolved to do the same thing. It was easy enough to accomplish, and it seemed like the right thing to do, as my life was obviously over. I couldn't even hold a busboy job anymore, because I couldn't stay on my feet for a full shift. I couldn't survive without constant doses of alcohol. I was in the final stage of the illness, so I would drink for a few hours, sleep for few hours, and then wake up and drink again.

I'd tried to detox myself once the last time I was in San Francisco, about a year or so earlier. I'd gotten myself into a god-awful little hole of a room above a strip joint on Broadway, and I planned to wait out the demons. I lay in the bed with torn sheets and blankets, sweating and shaking and hearing voices.

My room had a window that looked out on an air shaft, and I watched it go dark at night and brighten in the morning—and so I counted the hours of my agony. After two days and two nights of muscle spasms, diarrhea, and fitful bouts of non-sleep, I was getting dehydrated, so I walked down the dirty stairwell to the street like a zombie. It must've been 3 a.m., but there was a little all-night store a few doors down were I could buy some orange juice. The shocker came when I saw a stack of the next day's newspapers sitting by the cash register. I couldn't believe it.

What the newspaper was telling me, by its awful, incomprehensible date, was that two days had not passed, but only a part of a day. I'd hallucinated the passing of time, and I was at the beginning of the detox, not the end. It was too much for me, and I returned the juice to the cooler and bought two quarts of beer instead. There was no escape and I never tried again.

I didn't know anything about addiction or recovery in those days. I figured I could probably stop drinking if I checked into a church mission of some sort and licked the boots of some priest for the next couple years, but I was a card-carrying atheist in those days and had been a philosophy major in college, so I could argue my points with vigor and depth. In better days, I liked nothing better than welcoming the Jehovah's Witnesses into my college apartment on a Saturday morning with a drink in one hand and a joint in the other, so I could demolish their puny beliefs in God. When I was growing up, I'd been an altar boy and had tried to believe as my father had, but all that was gone, and I embraced the intellectual fashions of the day.

As I sat in the park, planning my suicide, I resolved not to tell anyone. I wanted nothing but to be eliminated, to be erased from the face of the earth. I was obviously a loser, unable to write, unable to work, and unable to keep a girlfriend. I'd screwed up every chance I'd had in life, coming from a good home and a good family, but tossing it all away. I'd gone to college and done well, but then inexplicably skipped the finals and flunked all my classes. And so on—just because the booze and drugs called the tune and I liked the dance. In the last eight years, I'd ridden trains and buses and hitchhiked thousands of miles—ten thousand, I believe—but all to no purpose other than to outrun the wreckage I was making of my life. Now, there was no run left in me, no spark, no hope. Suicide seemed like a good idea, and I told no one about my plans. Perhaps I could get this one thing right, as hollow and sad as it seemed.

My penultimate act would be to have a one-man going-away party. I scrounged what money I could, bought a bunch of booze, and brought it back to my miserable flophouse room on Columbus Avenue. The small necessities required for my destruction were easy to be had, so now I would enjoy one last good drunk—a real corker—and then get down to business. I dimly remember carrying a large amount of alcohol up to my room, but beyond that I remember nothing, and I assume I drank myself into a roaring blackout. But apparently, while I drank and then slept, unseen forces were at work.

The next morning, I was startled awake by a loud banging on my door. "You've got a phone call," said someone, pounding on my door until I acknowledged. I opened my eyes and found myself fully clothed, laying crossways on the bed with the room in a terrible mess. I made my way up the hallway and down several flights of stairs to an old pay phone in the basement, with the receiver hanging down by its cord. I picked up the phone and said, "Hello?"

It was my father. As far as I knew, my parents didn't even know what state I was in, let alone the city, much less an address, and certainly not the number to a pay phone in the basement of this flophouse. It was 1981, long before the era of cell phones or Internet or any way of easily finding people, and I was shocked to hear his voice. Was I dreaming? My dad tried to talk to me, but I cut him off short and said, "I can't talk to you right now. I'll call back," and hung up.

I was busted. I didn't know how or by whom, but it was obvious that someone had spoken to my parents and told them how bad off I was. Did they have a private detective on the case? It wouldn't be the first time they'd tried to find me. I was depressed beyond speaking, as I had only wanted to kill myself in peace. I had been a failure at everything, and now, it appeared, I wasn't even going to be able to commit suicide properly. Like every other problem, the only obvious solution was to have a drink, so I headed off to Coit Liquor, just across the street and down the block, and bought a small bottle of wine. Then I crossed back over Columbus Avenue diagonally to Washington Square Park, sat down on the grass with my small brown paper bag, and started drinking.

It was about 9 a.m. on a weekday morning, and everywhere I looked I saw busy people going to work with their briefcases and business suits. Over in one corner of the park, a group of Chinese people was practicing tai chi, with slow, careful movements that twisted my brain like a chicken gizzard. And then there was me, twenty-six years old with a two-thousand-pound hangover, drinking warm red wine from a green bottle in a brown bag, and wondering what to do. The wine stunk like rotting fruit, but it was my only haven.

I couldn't focus on the businesspeople with their sense of purpose, or the tai chi people with their balance, or, for that matter, the sun in the sky, which was uncharacteristically showing itself between the racing clouds. All I could see was the thing I needed: the little green bottle in the brown paper bag. My whole life seemed to come down to this wretched flask. I looked down the neck of the bottle, down into the abyss of the bottle, into the black hole that was sucking my life down into oblivion, and then I did something I hadn't done since I was a boy: I started to cry.

I cried like a fool, sitting cross-legged in the grass in the middle of the park in broad daylight. I cried for the waste of my life, for the stupidity of my drinking, and for the final solution that now had to come, before anything else got in the way. I recovered myself quickly, embarrassed by my display of emotion, and resolved that I would go back to my room and take care of business. But I was paranoid. I was sure my parents had called the police, or were ready to call them, and they obviously knew where I was, so I had to get them off my back. Over in the other corner of the park was a kiosk that held several pay phones, so I walked over to call home, collect.

My mother answered the phone, and she was as warm and loving as ever, but she seemed in a hurry to give the phone to my father. He was measured and calm in talking with me, which was highly unusual during that time in my life. He loved me more than anything in the world, but I know I tried him like a gang of devils. We hadn't had many calm conversations in the last few years, and our anger and frustration had run high.

We talked for a brief moment and then he asked me a simple question. "Jeff," he said, "how are you doing?"

I was dumbfounded. How was I doing? My mouth hung open and then shut again without producing a sound. How was I doing? My brain was spinning and I didn't know what to say. I was sick as a dog, bleeding from both ends, and about to commit suicide. How was I doing? But the sun was shining, the birds were singing, and the church across the street was bathed in sunlight. How was I doing?

I don't know where the words came from, or why, or how, but I proceeded to say the single most intelligent thing I've ever said in my life.

"I think I need to go into a hospital," I said.

In no time at all, there was a taxicab, a bit of money, and a plane ticket. A doctor my parents had consulted had recommended that I be allowed to continue drinking until I was in medical hands, so I was happily ordering double scotches from the stewardess and landed in Detroit very well oiled. The next morning, my parents threw me in the back of the car and drove me to Hurley Hospital in Flint, eighty miles away, which was the closest detox bed available. I remained in that hospital for ten days, as I recall.

The first night in the hospital was horrible. There was a frail old alcoholic in the bed next to me who was delirious, and I think he may have died in the middle of the night. A few hours after lights out, a squad of nurses and doctors ran into the room and started working on him furiously. I kept my head turned away with my eyes closed. It sounded like gruesome things were happening, and sometime later things went quiet and they wheeled him out. I never saw the old man again.

The next day, I had a visit from the head doctor on the ward, Dr. William Keating, who had decades of experience in alcohol and drug treatment. I was a punk kid sitting on the side of the bed, shaking and sweating and feeling terrible. I was wearing a blue hospital gown that tied up in the back ineffectively. Dr. Keating strode into the room with authority—a big, powerful black man with a white coat, a stethoscope, and a clipboard. It was like God himself coming in to take charge. He pulled up a chair and got right up in my face and called out like he was trying to wake the dead. And maybe he did.

"Boy!" he said.

I almost jumped out of my skin.

"Boy," he said, "you've got a disease. You're not responsible for what you've done."

Great, I said to myself.

"But you're responsible for what you do now."

Shit, I said to myself.

"Your disease is incurable," he said. "The most we're going to be able to do is put it in remission. We're going to give you a program to follow: Twelve Steps. You follow that program and the disease will stay in remission. You stop following that program and the disease is going to kick you in the ass again."

Then he stood up and walked out.

I didn't know what he was talking about. I didn't know anything about alcoholism or AA or anything else, but I was suddenly alert in the daze of detox, and I tried to ponder his statements. As the hours and days went by, Dr. Keating's brief prognosis and prescription echoed in my mind, like operating instructions for a new life.

I still think of him as a giant, but when I saw the good doctor again some days later, I was surprised to find out he wasn't a big man with a booming voice. Rather, he was an older gentleman, short and slight, who moved with energy and purpose. He had a deep reservoir of what he called "hog-trough philosophy," a collection of homespun stories that he poured out in lectures to the assembled patients. I loved his common-sense approach, and I hung on to his words, convinced he had a solution that just might work. In the months that followed, everything Dr. Keating said proved right.

Back in the cockpit of *Lifeboat*, I came out of my reverie with a slight smile. This storm was nothing compared to those days, and I was determined to make it through. The wind had built up impressively through the night, and it wasn't just gusting anymore, but steadily blowing. This storm hadn't been predicted before I left, but then the only prediction I'd known about had been for Beaufort, now eighty miles behind me. I was clearly sailing into a full-blown December gale that was just hitting its stride and probably settling in for days.

I was exhausted from wrestling the boat all night, but grateful that the Aries was finally working properly. Uncontrolled jibes could dismast a sailboat in this kind of storm, and dismasting could easily result in sinking. But as long as the Aries held, *Lifeboat* and I would keep plowing along.

There was nothing more for me to do, so I got up from the rain-soaked cockpit and headed down to the pilot berth for some rest. Dr. Keating was a great believer in "doing the next right thing" and avoiding "analysis paralysis," so I pulled off my boots, stripped off my foul-weather gear, and lay down. What pleasure I felt stretching out on that blessedly flat surface, my aching body consecrated by exhaustion. I was absurdly happy as I slid toward sleep—so delicious was that narrow berth, so wondrous my life.

CHAPTER 10

The Dream Machine

I woke up groggy a few hours later and stuck my head out the companionway hatch. It was late morning, but looked like dusk, with the rain scouring the cockpit and the clouds hunkered down for an all-day stink. The storm was blowing thirty-some knots, which is a hell of a sustained wind, and it showed no sign of letting up. *Lifeboat's* rigging seemed dangerously overloaded by the gale, so I put myself to the unpleasant job of reefing the mainsail again, even before having something to eat.

Reefing on *Lifeboat* meant being in two places at once. I had to ease the halyard on the mast to lower the sail and at the same time position myself on the boom to gather the sail, tie the reefing knots, and secure the excess canvas. At the mast, I had the advantage of standing on the deck, but hanging on to the boom called for dancing on the cabin top or balancing on the edge of the cockpit, all the while riding the roller coaster up and down the waves. I remembered the old rule: "Keep one hand for yourself and one for the ship," so you don't wind up in the drink.

The next order of business was to take down the big foresail and put up a smaller jib. Once again, a crew member should be on the halyard to lower the sail, and another crew on the foredeck to gather the sail, unclip it from the headstay, and bag it. If you just uncleat the halyard and let it run, it might jump the sheave at the top of the mast and jam. Also, the sail will fall down unabated to the deck and flail like a wild animal, and at least part of it might go overboard and transform itself into a sea anchor, possibly ripping the sail. Fortunately, I avoided the worst of these problems and got the sail down.

Then I had to sit up on the bow railing that ran around the tip of the boat and unhank all the brass shackles that held the sail in place. The sturdy aluminum tubing of the rail (called the bow pulpit) extended out just over the front of the boat and provided a little spot to lean against or sit on, facing backward to address the sail. The waves had built up to a considerable height now, so sitting out on the bow pulpit and hanging my butt over the water was a terrific ride. I always loved riding the tip of the boat up and down the great troughs, but I felt particularly vulnerable out here with the wind blowing so hard. There would be no one to do a man-overboard procedure if I fell in. The boat would simply sail away on its own, leaving me bobbing in waves. More than a few solo sailors had died that way.

Still, I loved the ride and I paused to really feel the roller coaster as the bow ran up the face of the waves, fell down into the troughs, and rose again. It was wild and dangerous, and I exulted in the moment, soaked with rain and holding onto the stay like a crazy man. Maybe I was headed for a Caribbean dream or maybe I was headed for trouble, but I was doing it, by God. I was doing something so mad and reckless that not one person in ten million would ever be foolish enough to try it, much less feel the glory of it. But I felt it now, sitting way out on the pulpit, riding the heart of the sea, plunging to its rhythm, soaring to its life. I felt the song of ten thousand years ringing through my sinews, the song that brings mad dreams to life.

When the sail was finally bagged and stuffed down the hatch, I had the pleasure of hoisting a smaller working jib and improvising the process in reverse. Something wasn't quite right with the halyard, and I was afraid it might be coming off its sheave at the top of the mast, but I got the job done and decided not to worry about it. There was nothing I could do about it anyway, and I could feel the weather deteriorating.

I was already regretting not choosing a smaller foresail, but I wanted to harness as much wind power as possible and make tracks for southern waters. Thirty knots is quite a strong wind (ten knots will hold a flag straight out), and the sails were now trimmed properly to take advantage of it, but I hated the thought of having to do it all again in a couple hours if the wind got any stronger.

Now that the sails were squared away, the problem of the boat's course demanded attention. I soon learned we were headed in the wrong direction. While I'd been sleeping, the wind had clocked around to the south, and since the Aries steered the boat *relative* to the wind, *Lifeboat* had turned with the wind. Instead of sailing southeasterly to cross the Gulf Stream, *Lifeboat* was now sailing southwesterly, back into the Gulf Stream—not to mention the fact that the Gulf Stream had been pushing us north at three knots or more per hour.

So *Lifeboat* and I hadn't been sailing southeasterly at all. This wasn't obvious until I checked the compass heading, because there aren't any landmarks in the middle of the ocean. I was far too poor to afford the kind of electronic devices that might have automatically corrected such problems. I couldn't even afford a generator.

A southerly wind, if it held, would slow my progress considerably. After I completed my transit of the Gulf Stream, I needed to head south for the Straits of Florida, but a sailboat can't sail directly into the wind. Not even close. A sailboat must always sail at an angle to the wind in order to catch the wind's power. Most sailboats like mine couldn't come closer than about forty-five degrees to either side of the wind, so if the wind was out of the south, I could sail southeast or southwest but not true south. If this wind continued to hold, I'd have to tack back and forth and back and forth to make headway, almost doubling the distance I'd have to sail.

At least I wasn't freezing. The Gulf Stream and the southerly gale brought warm air with the rain, so I didn't need many layers. I wasn't happy with my position, but on the other hand, I was quietly pleased with myself. One of my unspoken fears had been the prospect of reefing and changing sails in the middle of a storm, and now I'd done it, without a hitch. It was a good start, but I still had many miles to go. I wasn't cocky, but I shared a little smile with the great spirit of the universe.

A wind of thirty-some knots and gusting was manageable, but I couldn't take much more than that by myself. Too many things could go wrong. Daylight would be gone in a few hours, and I didn't want to be changing sails in the middle of the night. The wind was gaining strength, punishing the boat as I tried to sail close to the wind. My mainsail was double-reefed, and the working jib was doing her best, but when the wind momentarily roared past forty, my faith in the Aries wore thin. I couldn't afford to repeat the calamities of the night before.

Later in the afternoon, I decided to take defensive action and heave to, which is a way to take a break from active sailing and get some sleep or attend to other problems. When a boat is hove to, its forward momentum is all but stopped and the vessel is pointed mostly into the wind. This is done by backwinding the foresail and putting the rudder hard over. When done properly, the boat will sail right into the zone where it loses forward momentum and pretty much stay there.

It took almost an hour to get everything the way I wanted it, but I was well satisfied with the result. The wind piped up and the waves rolled by like hills in a moving car, but *Lifeboat* and I safely heaved to and floated along easily. Dusk was beginning to fall, though; without looking at my watch, it was hard to discern the change in the dank storm.

Out of the haze, I saw a ship about a half mile away, which was the very limit of my visibility. It wasn't a freighter, so I got out my binoculars to check it out. After a moment, I was able to discern that it was a Coast Guard cutter, and it had almost come to a stop. It dawned on me that I'd probably appeared on their hypersensitive radar, and they'd swung by to take a look. I suspect they were more than a little surprised to see a single-handed yacht way out here, especially in December, and they probably wondered what the hell I was doing.

I heard a crackling on my VHF radio and realized they were trying to hail me. The damned radio didn't seem to be working right, and I couldn't quite make out what the Coastie was saying, but I finally figured out they were asking if I wanted assistance. I told them I was OK, but they didn't seem to get the transmission, so I repeated it a few times. I couldn't tell what was wrong with my radio, but they got the message after a while and steamed away. Part of me wondered whether I might need assistance, and watching them disappear into the storm made me feel more alone than ever. But I was preoccupied with the mystery of the malfunctioning radio, and I started fiddling around with the wires, as I'd done the installation myself months ago.

For dinner I ate a bowl of hot stew in the rain, defying the waves as they receded into the darkness. I couldn't see them after nightfall, but the wind seemed louder, and I imagined they were building. Every now and then the deck would be awash with water or an immense gust would blast me with spray, but it was no worse than Lake Huron and a lot milder than the big storm we'd ridden out one night near the Straits of Mackinac. Still, as the last light faded away, I knew the night would be desolate.

In the dark, the waves were ominous, but I put them down in my logbook as purely average. This was a transparent lie, which I told myself for comfort. In fact, I couldn't calculate anything (other than the time, which was 6:30 p.m.) and couldn't see anything unless I used a flashlight or burned up battery power on the spreader lights. I just wanted to get this long leg to Florida over with. If the wind didn't shift to a better direction, it could take me twice as long to make West Palm Beach. But there was no way to avoid these hours and days now, whatever the weather might bring. I could only go through them, one gust at a time.

It was the same way in treatment. As I came to the end of my stay at Hurley Hospital, I considered the recommendation of the staff: twenty-eight more days at a residential treatment center. It seemed like an ungodly amount of time, and I initially balked. What would I do for twenty-eight days, or, more importantly, what would they do to me?

An old man by the name of Zeb came from outside the hospital to lead an AA meeting with a handful of patients, and I reluctantly joined the group. He had white hair and fiery blue eyes, with the trim figure of a man half his age. We sat around in a circle of chairs, and I wondered what was going to happen. It was my first time.

"My name's Zeb, and I'm an alcoholic," he said. "I drank for twenty years, and I've been sober for twenty years, and there ain't nothing about this shit I don't know."

I liked him immediately. He reminded me of the old farts I used to drink with in street corner bars, the kind who didn't give a damn what anybody thought. But Zeb was different. He was spry and healthy and quick as a wink, like a sly fox playing with a leash of cubs. There was a joy in his eyes, but also an awareness, like someone who'd lived to tell a tale.

It turned out that Zeb knew one of the patients in the group, an older guy in hospital pajamas, sitting right next to me.

"Harry!" said Zeb. "What in the hell are you doing here?"

"Well," said Harry, "I was sober for seven years . . ."

My head bucked and I turned to look at the man.

"I was sober for seven years," he said, talking like his mouth was full of oatmeal. "Well, and then I cut down on my meetings. And then I quit going to meetings. And then I had a drink. And then I had a whole bunch of drinks, and pretty soon I was worse off than I ever was before."

Damn, I thought, *the disease kicked him in the ass again, just like the doctor said.*

Zeb didn't give him a hard time, which surprised me. I thought Zeb was going to do an Uncle Randy on him, but he said only a few gentle words. His approach managed to magnify the poor guy's lesson for the rest of us, as though it were Exhibit One in the school of alcoholism, while soothing Harry's shame with a balm of compassion. I'd never seen anything quite like it.

In the Hurley Hospital days of funky blue gowns and foam slippers, I was grateful to be in a clean bed and eating three meals a day. I was positively thrilled to have a solid bowel movement, as opposed to the constant diarrhea of my addiction. Healing was possible, I realized. Change was possible. I decided to take Dr. Keating's advice and go to the twenty-eight-day program at a treatment center called Maplegrove.

By the time I arrived, I was in better physical shape and I came willingly. But within a day or two, I was off on an emotional roller coaster, pleading to leave treatment every chance I got. I was glad to be there one minute and wanted to leave the next. The staff would get me calmed down, and then I'd want to leave again. Somehow, I kept agreeing to give it one more day and ultimately got past the worst of the mood swings. But my brain still spun at an alarming rate, churning out thoughts that were pure sabotage. Food helped, along with physical exercise, which led to the gift of sleep.

I brought my shallow grandiosity into the group therapy sessions, either telling war stories of cross-country binges or needlessly complicating the basic concepts of recovery. Part of me wanted to take the simple wisdom to heart, but my pride was too great and my stake in intellectual fashion was too deep. I couldn't imagine the smart set subscribing to slogans such as "Easy Does It" or "Let Go and Let God," and I wasn't buying any of that drivel, either. I'm sure the counselors saw me racing straight for a relapse, but I was glad to entertain the other patients with my stories. Only rarely did I catch sight of my insanity, my loneliness, and my fear, and I had no more idea what to do with those things than would a newborn baby.

Most of the lectures in treatment were boring, so I was delighted when Dr. Keating came down from Flint to give a talk. What a giant this slight little man was! He talked about keeping things simple and taking the small actions necessary to get things done.

"Do you want to go downtown?" he asked. "Then get off the couch, check the bus schedule, walk to the corner, get on the downtown bus, put the fare in the box, take a seat, and ride."

He looked around the room to see if we got the point.

"But you have to get off the couch!" he said, pounding the podium.

"Do you want to recover?" he asked. "Get off the couch, check the meeting schedule, go to the meeting, and listen to other alcoholics who have stopped drinking. And do what they tell you to do."

His hog-trough philosophy was very attractive to me. Although he was a physician, he challenged us to reject people who merely studied addiction academically and instead advised us to follow people who'd conquered it personally.

"Do you want to learn how to skin a mule from somebody who read about it in a book?" he asked. "Or do you want to learn from a mule skinner?"

Bill Keating wasn't in recovery from any addiction himself, but like many doctors of that era, he had great faith in Twelve Step programs. He knew there was nothing in medicine to cure the insanity of addiction, but he saw that somehow alcoholics were able to help each other in the structure of the meetings. This leaderless group was straightforward, selfless, and free. What could be better? Dr. Keating's effectiveness was grounded in his ability to persuade us to put our swollen brains on the shelf and follow the program.

Small things mattered a lot to me in those fragile days. The first time I went into the dining hall at Maplegrove and saw freshly laundered tablecloths and shining silverware, I was overwhelmed. Simple kindness meant everything, and I understood in my better moments that the universe, along with the staff and my family, was being kind to me. I had been spared undeservedly and I knew it.

Three days a week we had relaxation class in the late afternoon, which was some of the best treatment I ever received. It seemed silly at first, but as I went along with the class, the exercise worked like a narcotic. I would lie on a green mat in a darkened room and follow the therapist's lead. First, tense the muscles in my feet, then release; tense the muscles in my calves, then release; tense the muscles in my thighs, my arms, my shoulders, and my back, then release, until all the muscle groups were relaxed, breathing in rhythm with the exercise. I just fell into the moment and breathed.

The exercises calmed the arguments in my skull and gave me a scant bit of help in learning how to sleep without alcohol. I loosened up, breathed in and out, and felt my exhaustion. During the classes, the instructor took us through a rudimentary meditation, and I allowed myself to follow. I could almost glimpse another world.

The days and weeks went by, and my parents attended the five-day family program, much to my amazement. We sat stoically through the family therapy and educational lectures, taking in as much as we could, but saying little. I remember sitting through a lecture on alcoholism and sexual dysfunction with my parents on either side, burning with humiliation. I felt like I was being held underwater, unable to think of anything but breaking free.

My parents drove more than an hour each way to attend the many meetings and lectures of the family program, their actions speaking a language I could barely understand. Dad put all his business affairs on hold to participate, which would double his burden in the weeks to come. Even I could appreciate his sacrifice, which he made silently in spite of his ongoing battle with leukemia.

My mother always brought joy with her, a wondrous balm for my struggles. It shone as the purest love, radiating from her beautiful blue eyes. Her unshakable faith in me, despite my years of deceit, gave me courage. She often surprised me with her wry wit.

"How are you doing today, my angel?" she'd ask.

"Fine," I'd say.

"Really?" she'd say, raising her eyebrows with dramatic flair.

I couldn't help but laugh. Whatever worries she had for me were buried deep down in her heart, so only the light shone through, like a beacon bringing me back to shore. I was ashamed of myself for being so rotten to them both. I wanted to do better.

My father brought me a new clock radio while I was there, called a Dream Machine. He'd already done so much for me that this kindness was unexpected. Through all the years I had with my father, I rarely comprehended how insightful and thoughtful he was until after his death. Little did I know at that moment, he would be gone in just over a year.

Remembering those days while on the rain-drenched cockpit of *Lifeboat* was difficult, and I looked out into the unfathomable darkness of the storm. It seemed as though I'd sailed into a black nebula, roiling in another region of time and space. There was no future in the darkness, only a screen to play memories on, and I continued into the past, even as the present storm threatened my boat.

During the waning days of my treatment at Maplegrove, I had come close to disaster. One dank and fateful afternoon, I'd taken a walk that turned into a crisis. In many ways, it was just like the storm—unexpected and inescapable. But unlike the storm, it was exactly the kind of crisis I needed.

CHAPTER 11

A Desperate Situation

A few days before the end of my treatment at Maplegrove, the obsession to drink came on me again. I was walking around the grounds in the November chill, oppressed by the low-slung clouds, and thinking about what I'd do and where I'd go after discharge. Maybe I could stay with my old girlfriend in New York, if she'd have me. Maybe I could go out West, get a little job, and concentrate on writing. Or go back to college and actually finish. I walked the grounds of the treatment center, thinking about the options, when I was abruptly confronted by a stark fact: *I was going to drink again.*

It wasn't a stray thought or a vague possibility; it was a certainty, as though I'd just caught sight of an approaching storm, with thunderheads that spanned the horizon, too big to avoid and pointless to deny.

I'm going to drink, I said to myself.

I was repelled by the statement, but its truth was irrefutable. It echoed in my mind again involuntarily, though the words sickened me.

I'm going to drink.

It was a terrible idea, I knew, but there was no avoiding it. The consequences would be awful, but I was trapped. I knew what I was going to do, if not in the details, then in the result. An obsession can be delayed, but not denied.

I wanted to escape, to free myself from the snare, but it was too late. I had no desire to drink, in a way, no wish to plunge my life back into darkness, but I had to drink. I was going to drink, just as surely as I was going to breathe again in the next few seconds. The overthrow was complete. The compulsion owned me in a way my conscious mind couldn't fight.

I tried to reason with myself, to assure myself that I was in control of my own destiny, but it was no use. I could argue with myself all I wanted. I could run through all the cognitive exercises I'd been taught. But deep down I knew—and knew for certain—that I would drink again very soon. It was depressing and hateful and wrong, but it was unavoidable.

Then another fact became obvious, with the same icy clarity: *I'm going to die*. I could see these two facts as clearly as I could see the fingers on my right hand. They were as simple and undeniable as childhood arithmetic: two plus two equals four. *I'm going to drink again and I'm going to die.*

The statement repeated itself relentlessly, as though a judge were pronouncing a death sentence over and over again inside my skull. I wondered at the madness of it. I was my own judge, jury, and executioner. I wanted no part of it, but the wheels kept turning.

I'm going to drink again and I'm going to die.

I wasn't being melodramatic, either. My drinking and drugging had led me into some brutal places over the last few years. I remembered being beaten to a pulp and thrown headfirst down a long flight of stairs by a leather-clad biker. I remembered spinning out of control on the freeway and being hit broadside by a semi. I remembered ingesting more than twenty drops of liquid LSD by accident and nearly losing my mind. So many close calls, but there would be no lucky break this time. My time was up and there was no reprieve. I was going to drink, and it would not go well. The death sentence kept repeating itself in my head.

I'm going to drink again and I'm going to die.

And wouldn't it be simple justice? Wouldn't it be fair? There was obviously something rotten in me, something that needed to be thrown out in the trash. It was shameful after all my parents had done to save me, all the time and money they'd spent to put me on my feet again. Truly, I wasn't worth saving.

I schemed to find a way out, a safe haven where I could begin again with a minimum of danger. I'd go stay with Helen in New York, or Lisa, wherever she was. I could always go back to Atlanta or Chicago, or maybe try a new city. But no matter what story I tried to sell myself, the refrain continued in my head.

I'm going to drink again and I'm going to die.

There was no arguing the facts. I walked around the grounds searching for a way out, but there was nothing but gloom and the endlessly repeating statement. When the cold became too oppressive, I went back inside, but I avoided people and conversation.

In my mind, the stream of memories continued, framing my inevitable fate in the light of past experience. I remembered what it was like to be hungry and penniless in a great American city, to walk down the street, past the little markets and restaurants, with an empty wallet. I remembered the violent drunks and the weapons that filled the night. I'd seen how fast things got ugly, how it happened in a flash, like a dogfight. I knew intuitively that when I started drinking again, the gift of my deliverance would be withdrawn.

I felt certain I wouldn't see my twenty-seventh birthday, now less than two months away. I didn't know if I'd be shot or stabbed or just get too sick to live. But I knew I'd wind up broke again and find myself in the wrong place at the wrong time.

All the rest of the afternoon and into the evening, my internal verdict was endlessly repeated. *I'm going to drink again and I'm going to die.* All through dinner and the small talk with other patients, all through the miscellaneous evening activities, I found no relief. I told no one about my torment, and I walked away from the TV room so I could think.

I became desperate to find a solution, a way out. I felt trapped by the inevitability of it all and breathless with anxiety. My mouth was dry as I walked the hallways, and I stuffed my hands deep into my pockets. My former resolve and determination were meaningless. There was defeat in the refrain now and a cold patina of fear.

I'm going to drink again and I'm going to die.

Time dilates in a terrible way during a bad car accident. In the last seconds before impact, you can see it all coming. The crash is unavoidable and it's happening too fast to shield yourself or make a different choice. You only have time to gasp—not even to scream. I was trapped in that last second before impact all evening and deep into the night, hour after hour. The refrain was my only companion.

Maybe the internal bleeding would begin again, weakening me to the point where my capillaries would burst for good. Maybe I'd just kill myself, like I'd been planning to do. The details didn't matter since the conclusion was the same. Images kept flashing in my mind. I wriggled helplessly in a web of despair, waiting for the black widow.

I left the common areas, closed the door to my room, and sat alone all night. I was desperate to find a solution and went to the window, trying to look into the future, but the glass only reflected my image back to me. I was superfluous, unnecessary. I turned away and paced the room, alternately sitting and standing. It was late. I tried to read, but soon threw the book aside, unable to focus on the words. It was a lonesome time, and the halls outside my door went quiet. There was only me and the bed and a simple desk with a chair. My world had collapsed into a small, carpeted room with a few books on the windowsill and a clock radio. I had no hope and could almost feel the approaching impact, my muscles tensing involuntarily.

I would leave treatment and take off for the West Coast. I'd probably hitchhike the interminable distance across the States until I wound up in a North Beach flophouse again, in a tiny room that reeked of smoke and ruin. I would get myself into a place where I could drink and drug and be left alone. I saw how my parents' hearts would break; I saw the anger of my siblings and friends, the brew of negative emotions that would send me over to the other side of the continent.

Just so I could drink! I was amazed by the insanity of it, but I couldn't break free. It was not a choice or a lack of insight or a shortage of willpower. I was being pulled out to sea by a riptide of compulsion, a power greater than myself, and I knew that there was no hope of swimming when the sea itself is against you. But I didn't want to give up either.

Lifeboat was being pushed to the limit, even with a reefed mainsail. I had too much canvas up, the wind was too strong, and I was too exhausted to change the headsail again. Although the boat was hove to, the working jib was too big for the job, and it was yanking the boat around violently. My plan for an easy night had gone to hell. I hadn't expected a storm like this and I wasn't fully prepared for it. The radio wasn't working right and the bilge pump had quit. Fortunately, the boat didn't seem to be taking on much water, so at least that wasn't going to sink me. Yet.

But could the boat take this continuous punishment? If not, there was little hope for me. I had a small dinghy riding about twenty feet behind the boat, attached by a line called a painter. Towing the dinghy was a good idea in fair weather, but a foolish arrangement in these conditions. If I'd planned more carefully, I would've lashed the dinghy upside down on the foredeck before I left, to keep it secure. As it was, I expected the brave little dink to be torn away at any moment. That little plastic tub wasn't much comfort, but the dinghy was my only escape capsule. I checked with my flashlight to see if it was still there.

My eyes returned to the binnacle and the rain beating against the faintly illuminated globe of the compass. It was time to think through the worst-case scenario. After all, if the boat were dismasted in the next two minutes, I couldn't be surprised. If the hull were punctured and the sea rushed in, I'd need to reel in the dinghy and climb aboard with a flashlight, a life jacket, and whatever food I could grab. But who would even report me missing? And could I even make it into the dinghy from a sinking boat in twenty-foot waves? And what good would it do to be floating in a storm in a six-foot plastic rowboat? It was a desperate situation. I could easily die tonight, and no one would know it for quite some time.

But then I remembered something my old girlfriend Holly had said to me once. I was sober a bit longer than she was, but we were both fairly new in recovery and just getting our bearings. We'd been walking through a quiet neighborhood among tall trees on a late fall afternoon, and I'd been venting my frustrations about something or other. I don't remember her saying much while I carried on about my problems, but finally she squeezed my hand and got my attention.

"But you know," she said.

The silence hung in the air for a moment and she turned to me.

"You're all right, right now."

It was a minor revelation, and as the leaves swirled and the sun went low in the sky, I saw things as they really were. A lightness came over me as we continued to walk along, and I laughed out loud. I was all right, *right now.*

Lifeboat was being hammered by the waves and I could hardly stand in the cockpit, so the situation was far different from that afternoon walk, but I came to the same realization: I was all right, right now. After all, the Aries was keeping its course, the rigging was holding up the mast, and the hull was still sound. The storm was going to do its worst, no matter what, but I'd done everything I could, and the things that weren't all right were well beyond my control. If I was going to have any chance of survival, I needed to get some rest.

The cabin down below was a mess, but easy to ignore in the dark, so I stepped over the debris and wedged myself into the pilot berth. I laid down soaking wet and fully dressed in my foul-weather gear, ready to abandon ship, if necessary. It was deafening down below, between the thrashing of the boat, the beating of the waves, and the roaring of the wind. I was prepared for the worst, but I closed my eyes just the same. I didn't expect to sleep, but a few moments' rest would help.

My brother Greg (left) and me, about 1985, when I came out to visit him in San Diego.

My father, Bob Jay, sailing with Fred Jensen about 1952, before Fred became commodore of the Detroit Yacht Club.

Sailing *Lifeboat* in Lake Huron the summer before I began the journey. What could go wrong?

Mary Butler sitting on Rosie, her mobility scooter, about 1989. It probably took 3 hours for her aid to help her get ready.

Lifeboat at rest further along in the journey, about 8 months after the storm.

My portrait of Mom and Dad
(Robert Janiga Jay and Sara Critton
Jay) at home, about 1971.

Mom and Dad sailing (probably on
Uncle Randy's mahogany boat *Yawl's
Rebel*) about 1952.

Sitting at the dinette in *Lifeboat's* saloon
some months after the storm, 1991.

At the wheel of *Lifeboat*, summer 1990.

CHAPTER 12

Revelation

The drinking obsession gripped me all through that terrible night at Maplegrove, and I couldn't get free of it. Reading was impossible and sleep was out of the question. The knowledge that I would drink again, the certainty of it, and the vision of where drinking would take me scoured out my guts and shrunk my heart.

I kept trying to convince myself logically that it was avoidable, that I could do something different or that I could go to a safe place. But geographical cures had always been my solution in the past, and I always wound up in the same quagmire. Would this time be different? I'd learned a few things in treatment, and perhaps those things could help me, but I didn't buy the spiritual stuff. Deep in my mind was a hunger that wouldn't be denied, and *that* was my Higher Power.

The ebb tide of addiction was carrying me out to sea, and I could see how it would swallow me down to ten thousand feet, where no light could penetrate. I didn't believe in anything, but I was sober long enough at this point—more than a month—to have a real and natural fear of death. When one is actively drinking and drugging, there is no fear of death. Extinction looms on the horizon like an oasis of peace, a release from madness. Not only is death inevitable, it is just and proper. An addict lives with the specter of death like a long-overdue electric bill, waiting for the lights to go out.

But I hadn't had a drink in weeks. I was getting my health back, eating three meals a day, and sleeping without chemicals. I wasn't exactly on a pink cloud, but I was on the mend. When I'd first entered the hospital,

I'd felt like an old man, but now I was starting to feel the vigor of my age and I had hope for a new life. I didn't want to die. I didn't want to end my young life as a midnight statistic on a city street. I wanted to live. But the riptide of addiction was pulling me out into the night, a night that had only one end: mine.

This anguish lasted for hours, with the unavoidable truth always in my head: *I'm going to drink again and I'm going to die.* I was frantic to break its grasp and hopeless at the same time. I paced the small room, sat in the desk chair, and stared at the window. I didn't believe in hell, but I was in it, burning in my own helplessness and fear. The hours and minutes glowed on the face of the Dream Machine like an inscrutable countdown.

People in recovery talk about desperation as a gift, because it strips away the intellect and lays the choices bare. Desperation brings clarity to the mind by tearing away the comforts of arrogance and pride. It rips away the shield of self-pity and depression, and calls for a decision. Sink or swim! The gift of desperation is the last chance for life. It is the gift of grace.

This agony made me do something I'd never done before, something I never would've done under any other circumstances. And out of this simple action came all my recovery. At about two o'clock in the morning, I got down on my knees in the middle of the room. I was beyond hope, beyond words, beyond anything I'd ever known.

I knelt down on the carpet, held my hands in prayer, and cried out to the one I didn't believe in.

"God, help me," I said.

Then I buried my face in my hands and sank into the darkness and pleaded, "God, help me."

I knelt in the ruins of my life, alone. I closed my eyes against the void, drained of all expectation. Yet within me was the slightest glimmer of hope, like an echo from the past, and in that moment of supreme desolation, I was lifted up and something happened that I can only explain in the way a child might explain it: all of heaven opened up for me.

A kind of waterfall seemed to be breaking over me, a waterfall of love. I was kneeling under a great, cleansing waterfall that came in wondrous torrents. It was water made of light, pure and silky. It was alive, too, and personal. It wasn't a substance, but a living presence, wiser and more intuitive than I could grasp. This presence was greater than the world, yet flowing into the world, and washing over me and filling me with joy. I knew I was in the presence of Christ.

We knew each other as friends know one another, but deeper than that, deeper than I knew my own thoughts. And this cascade poured over my mind and washed away all my fears and doubts. And I knew it would always be with me, whenever I opened my heart.

The joy of meeting was ecstatic and spacious. My fear of death, my inability to control myself, my nameless anxieties and torments were all obliterated. And I knew I could stay sober. I was in a rapture, completely immersed in the heart of God and swept into eternity.

I could also see that God had no more in common with our religions than the ocean has with a small bay. The ocean may fill the bay, and the bay may hold some fraction of the ocean, but they are utterly different. Every wondrous thing attributed to God is true, but in this life we are only at the edge of the bay and we can't see the waters beyond. For a few moments though, I was alive in the ocean, the Divine exploded over me like an enormous surf, and I rode the boundless waves.

Under this endless cascade of love, still on my knees, but with my arms outstretched and looking up with wonder, I was transformed. My mind was unshackled and released into a greater realm. Not only did I know I could stay sober, I knew that all my malignant thoughts were illusions, and these illusions only lived on the power I gave them. All my demons were flushed downstream like motes of dust, entirely insignificant, and I was immersed in the water of life. We children have no vocabulary for this Love and its dominion, but my heart could feel it, and my heart rejoiced in it.

This presence was vastly powerful too. It populated the galaxies with stars and brought molecules to life. I saw that for God, creating a sparrow or creating a universe was just as easy, and each contained the other. There was no order of difficulty for God, only love. And this love was now streaming through me and washing out every foul thing that stood in its path.

I was released from the simple justice that condemned me and raised out of the void. It was so much more than I deserved, so outlandish, so wonderful that I did cartwheels through the universe. This was the amazing grace sung about in spirituals, and I had been the wretch—the most worthless of them all. But now the transformation was complete, and my joy was all the greater for being undeserved. I was made whole again purely out of love, and this love was boundless and infinitely creative. I could see it was the very womb from which the universe—and all of us—were constantly being born, new and vital, into each consecutive moment.

The rapture went on and on, for what I think was almost half an hour. Paradoxes opened into clarity, and mysteries became self-evident. I could see that evil and fearful things were meaningless because they were earthly, and the earth would pass away. Suffering was real enough, as I well knew, but it was finite, a string of dissonant notes in a grand symphony.

I saw then that only Love was infinite and eternal, and the darkness had no power against light, since it was only lack of light. Our little world, our current reality, would pass soon enough. But we would not, because we were children of light. Our place ultimately wasn't here, though we were fortunate to experience this life. Our experience on earth could be both terrible and majestic, but we were privileged beyond comprehension to be here with one another.

As the rapture wound down, I became overwhelmed and got up from my knees to lie down on the bed. Again and again I said, "Thank you," and knew I was heard. I knew I was always heard.

I was stupefied by the transformative power of what I experienced. It rewired my brain instantaneously and positively, in the same way a traumatic event can rewire the brain negatively. There was no dread left in my heart, no doubt in my mind. I was completely free of the obsession to drink and free of the heckling thoughts. I watched the fading light of this presence like the most beautiful sunset. Oh, those precious moments when the veil is lifted. How clear and fine they are!

Ultimately the rapture closed and the glow subsided. I found it jarring to move around the room and get ready for bed. The normal routine seemed clumsy compared to the greater Reality that had just been revealed to me, and my body seemed strange and mechanical. I was exhausted and slept deeply until the call for breakfast, which came too soon.

I told no one about my experience, either the next day or for many months. In fact, I was confused and conflicted and had a hard time adjusting my thinking. The daily schedule at the treatment center seemed disjointed, but only because I couldn't adjust myself to the ordinary flow of people and conversation. The puny nature of my character was beginning to reassert itself, too, and I was afraid of what people might think of me. I couldn't talk about my experience because it didn't fit into my worldview as an intellectual. Yet there was no denying its authenticity. By contrast, the physicality of the world seemed flimsy. I was disoriented, but with a little smile pulling at the corner of my mouth. I kept quiet.

One uncomfortable aspect of the situation was the fact that I'd proclaimed myself an atheist with great passion, and if there was one thing I didn't like, it was the giddy, born-again Christian. I couldn't make peace with fundamentalists or proselytizers of any religion. And I still couldn't. But there was no denying I'd had a firsthand experience of Immanuel—of "God with us"—and I'd seen how He could create and destroy with love and ease, if not by a biblical wave of the hand.

But perhaps a biblical wave of the hand was just as good a metaphor as anything else, since words were so inadequate. I couldn't describe my experience in words any more than I could describe the notes of a symphony. Who was I to disparage someone else's attempt? We are all infants. The disconcerting thing was I now knew what these religious types meant, and I could appreciate the universality of spiritual experience, whether it was a Sufi mystic, a Buddhist monk, or a Carmelite nun.

The more I thought about it, the more incredible it was. I had come to believe we are fashioned with minds and spirits that can glimpse the splendor, but it is always just out of reach, so in the clear light of day, a leap of faith is required. Whether one is an atheist or a believer, God is intellectually incomprehensible, like eternity or infinity. God can be fully revealed, but only to the soul, and the language of the soul was faith—and love.

I also knew then that the Eternal is always present, always available, always becoming in the same way that the next moment of time was always becoming. In fact, I realized that the Eternal is where the next moment of time comes from.

I didn't know anyone who would understand, or perhaps my pride was just too great to risk embarrassment. I didn't feel comfortable with religious people, and yet I now knew that a purely rational approach to life was incomplete. My encounter with God had been the most real experience of my life, but now I had to fit it into my everyday world, and I wasn't sure how to do it.

I couldn't wait for the day to be over, so I could get back to my room, alone. I was impatient with breakfast, lunch, and dinner, with the lectures, group therapy, and relaxation exercises. I just wanted to get back to my room, get down on my knees, and recreate the whole wonderful experience again.

Finally, the day was done and there would be nothing more to do. It felt good to close my door and prepare my mind for another session. I was expecting to have my own private time with the Eternal. I got down on my knees and started in.

"God help me," I said, meaning it.

Nothing happened. I prayed with more feeling. Nothing happened. I implored God and Jesus and the Holy Spirit to come to me. Nothing happened, or rather nothing spectacular. Maybe a little nudge, a celestial wink. What the heck was that?

I got off my knees and sat on the side of the bed. I was beginning to see. On the previous night, I'd had the most unforgettable experience of my life, but I wasn't going to be able to summon this cosmic light show for my own personal entertainment. I was embarrassed before God, but I sensed his amusement too. I was such a child.

One thing was obvious: I was going to have to work the Twelve Steps, just like Dr. Keating and Zeb and the counselors had been trying to tell me. I could begin to see how it all fit together, how it worked.

I could see I was going to recover from my alcoholism and drug addiction, but it wasn't going to happen overnight, and I was only at the beginning. I'd been given a reprieve from the demons, but I also had free will, and I could entertain my compulsions anytime I chose. I'd been given a glimpse of a greater reality, but I had to make my way through the physical world, with all its highs and lows. My intellect wasn't always going to be my ally on this journey, but my heart knew right from wrong, and I believed I could make it. From that day forward, I used the prayer "God help me" to beat back the darkness, and it never failed. If I had to say it a dozen times to cleanse my mind, that's what I would do, until the danger was past.

I used to think Reason was king and the spiritual realm was hogwash, but I now had a broader perspective. My experience had proven the two weren't separate, and, ironically, the intellect was really just a component of Spirit, along with intuition, creativity, and compassion. The intellect, for all its usefulness and power, was limited.

Gone were the immature conceptions of God that were so easily attacked by the rational mind. It was hilarious to even say something like "conceptions of God." A human mind couldn't comprehend infinity, much less God—any more than a cocker spaniel could understand quantum mechanics.

Yet I'd had that ineluctable experience, and those rapturous moments taught their own lessons. Some of those precious filaments remained, but more were hard to grasp, always slipping away like the threads of a dream. They returned more clearly when I tried not to understand.

"The way that can be spoken isn't the eternal way," wrote Lao-tzu.

"I am who am," said the burning bush to Moses.

There was no way to define these things—and no need to. I could feel "God with us" in the meetings, flowing through the stories, the laughter, and the pain. It was a miracle constantly being renewed, a gift. Einstein said, "When the solution is simple, God is answering." I knew where I needed to go.

The clinical staff at Maplegrove thought my newfound love of recovery was phony. I'd been coasting along through treatment, a typical hotheaded twenty-something. Now I was carrying on about the Steps like an old-timer and hijacking all the discussions with my own enthusiastic expositions. I still wasn't telling anybody about the depth of my spiritual experience, because I didn't want to be branded a fanatic. In fact, I didn't tell anyone about my experience for quite a long time.

But I never drank or drugged again. I became a regular at meetings, drank too much coffee, and laughed a lot. I discovered, much to my surprise, that I was already a pro at "One day at a time." During my drinking days, I'd never worried about next week's booze, and so I stopped worrying about next week's sobriety. I charged into recovery with a devil-may-care attitude and boundless faith. I was on fire.

CHAPTER 13

The Bow Pulpit

The storm was so loud that night and the boat's movement so jarring that sleep seemed out of the question. I needed to rest a bit though, so I stretched out on the narrow bunk in my foul-weather gear and closed my eyes, some time after midnight. I didn't think I'd actually nod off, but apparently I did, because an instant later—or what seemed like an instant—I was jolted awake by broad daylight. One minute I was lying down and the next I was waking up at 9 a.m. I jumped out of the berth and poked my head up the companionway to get a look around.

The rain had stopped, but the clouds were still heavy and blocked any direct sunlight. The wind and waves were as bad as ever, but they seemed less threatening now that I could see them. And besides, sweet old *Lifeboat* had made it through the night and was taking everything the gale could throw at her. I was so glad to see it all, to breathe the salty air, to feel the quickness of life. It was morning in hell, but all was well.

The freshness of a good night's sleep cleared my mind, and I was ready for work. There were lots of jobs to do around the boat, but none were urgent. So I struck a big kitchen match, lit the gimbaled stove, and made myself a full breakfast. I felt like an old sea dog, standing under the companionway hatch and frying up bacon, eggs, and potatoes in a cast-iron skillet. The spattering grease and the steaming percolator spread an aroma of humanity through the cabin.

I took my plate and coffee up to the cockpit and sat against the cabin side to protect my food from the wind. It was a dreary scene, but despite the god-awful weather, it was one of the most enjoyable breakfasts I could remember. The sheer joy of being alive was intoxicating, and every bite of food and sip of coffee seemed like the most exotic gift. My heart was light even as my mind wondered how we'd survived the night.

After finishing the meal, I refilled my coffee and stood in the well of the cockpit, surveying the boat from stem to stern. I still had too much sail up, that was clear. I needed to further reef the main or strike it altogether. I also needed to set my smallest storm jib, so I could ride out the storm for a day or two. Being hove to was problematic though, as the Gulf Stream would keep pushing me north if I wasn't making headway. But it was more important to survive than to make miles south, so I surrendered to the facts. Acceptance is easier with a full stomach.

I only hoped the wind wouldn't blow any stronger, as many sailors have had their boats dismasted by having too much sail up. I remembered being in an overnight race on Lake St. Clair when the wind piped up over thirty knots as the sun set. A couple of Can-Am racers were visiting our circuit from New York, and they scoffed at the idea that our little lake could give them any trouble, despite what their wind gauges were telling them. As the night wore on and the New Yorkers carried full sail, one was dismasted and the other broached and nearly sank. They were saved by emergency tow vessels, while the rest of us struggled on to the finish line. Nature can be an unsentimental teacher, though there was little danger for the New Yorkers, with rescue boats nearby.

My position was much different, and I needed to formulate a plan for a worst-case scenario. If the mast broke, I would use my big bolt cutters to free the steel rigging, so the whole mess would slip overboard without puncturing the deck or hull. It would be a dangerous situation with a broken mast flailing in the stays and thousands of pounds of pressure running through the guide wires. I hoped I wouldn't have to face that nightmare and gulped down my last bit of coffee before getting busy.

Looking up the mast and off into the sky, I found my place on the watery face of the earth. Here was the dream as it was lived in the real world, working against the storm and living to tell the tale. It was a wild and wonderful thing to be 130 miles offshore, blown to bits, unable to make headway, possibly headed for disaster, but still sailing. It was the real deal and it was ugly, but it was all mine and I thanked God for the chance to live it.

My little dinghy was still riding dutifully behind the boat, strung out on the painter and crashing through the waves in fine form. Its hollow-walled construction gave it superior floatation, and the dink took everything the storm could throw at it. What a brave little soul it seemed, struggling all through the night and day. If only my prayers could be as strong as that line. But all the dinghy had to do was hold on for dear life. I had to get up on deck and do something about the sails. Working on the foredeck would be treacherous, and I resolved to take my time and try not to get washed over the side in the process.

Stepping up from the cockpit onto the heaving deck, I made my way to the mast to let the foresail down. I uncleated the halyard gingerly, preparing to ease it down, but nothing happened. The halyard lay limp in my hands, while the jib stood firm, not even dropping a quarter of an inch. The halyard was jammed in its sheave at the top of the mast, more than fifty feet above the deck, like a rope that's jumped off the wheel of a pulley.

I tried whipping the loose end, sending waves of force up the line to the top of the mast. I tried it to the left and to the right; I tried it fast and slow, swearing and not swearing, but nothing worked. For a time, I would send rhythmic, almost prayerful waves up the line; then I would lose it and start whipping furious waves of force, clacking the halyard against the mast. This went on forever.

Normally, when a halyard gets jammed, the only remedy is to go aloft in a bosun chair and get it back on its sheave. This is a two-man job, though: one guy sitting in the sling seat attached to another halyard and one guy grinding a winch to hoist him aloft. But even if I could've done it on my own, which is a difficult exercise in a calm harbor, the fury of the storm put this option out of reach. But there was another method I could try.

There are two halyards at the front of the mast: one for the headsail, which was jammed, and one for the spinnaker, the big colorful running sail that flies on a sunny day before the wind. The spinnaker halyard was unused, and if I crossed it under the jib halyard, I might be able to use it as a lever to pop the jammed halyard up onto its sheave.

I positioned the spinnaker halyard under the jammed halyard at the top of the mast and worked it. Forever and a day I worked it. I whipped huge waves of force up the spinnaker halyard that translated into nudges on the jammed halyard at the top. I stood on the foredeck, craning my neck until I thought my head would fall off. The rain came back, off and on, the wind blew monotonously, and the waves tried to knock me off my feet, but the rotten little jib halyard wouldn't budge. I just kept at it.

Finally, I felt a quarter inch give, just enough to know it moved. Thank God. I kept working the hell out of it and finally the jam broke, the jib halyard popped back on its sheave, and the foresail was once again under my control. I pulled it down, furled it quickly, and shoved the wet canvas down the foredeck hatch. Now it was time to put up the storm jib.

There is nothing easy about trying to hank on a new sail in bad weather, and even the act of getting the sail out of its bag was challenging. Twenty pounds of sailcloth with a line of brass hanks can be a nasty adversary in a gale, but I got the tack fastened down, got the bag down the hatch, and then started hanking the sail onto the headstay.

Normally, I would've sat out on the bow pulpit and faced backward to hank the sail on the headstay, but the wind and waves were too dangerous, so I crouched on the deck and tried to hank it on from a more secure position. It was no use. So I carefully swung my butt up onto the pulpit to get the job done more efficiently. It was an act of faith to hoist myself onto that aluminum tube frame, holding the headstay with one hand and the sail with the other. The distance from the top of a wave to the trough below was considerable, and my stomach floated up and down like a carnival ride. I braced myself against the bow pulpit, riding the big waves, and paused for a moment to glory in it.

How lucky I was to be caught in this wonderful dream, how crazy and delicious and fine. My face and hands dripped with salt water and rain, blowing sideways in the wind. Sitting out there was like perching on the front rail of a roller coaster, facing backward, and flying down a blind track. I was helpless to control the motion of the boat, but I was getting the sail on, one maddening brass hank at a time. In hell and high water, I was getting it done. Barring a sudden catastrophe, the storm jib would be up soon and then I could heave to properly and rest easy.

Riding the long undulations of the bow pulpit was exhilarating, and I hated to leave it for the safety of the cockpit. For here was life, the great struggle and grind of it, the small victories and their satisfactions. I wanted to ride the bow pulpit all day, defying the gale and having my way with the wind and waves. When I'd finished the job and snapped the halyard to the head of the sail, I lingered there for a windblown moment and felt some heaven rushing through it.

CHAPTER 14

Driving with Dad

Easing out of *Lifeboat*'s bow pulpit, I made my way to the mast and raised the storm jib. This small triangle of canvas is the perfect match for a gale, catching as much wind power as a large sail on lesser days. Once the short sail was in place, I backed it to the wind and the boat immediately started riding easier.

The deck was treacherous, and I moved carefully from one handhold to another as I headed back to the cockpit. The storm showed no signs of letting up, and it was now about two in the afternoon. The bleakness of the day reminded me of the god-awful January when my father lay in the hospital, struggling for his life. Like the pitiless squalls, his illnesses battered him relentlessly, with no hope for a quick ending.

He'd been sick with leukemia for years, with many hospitalizations and primitive treatments. There were no effective medicines at that time, so the doctors pumped him full of steroids and first-generation chemo drugs. In the end, he was diagnosed with heart disease too, and his doctors prescribed open-heart surgery. He lived less than nine months after that final assault. For some reason, the cancer that had metastasized around his spine wasn't identified until the very end.

On the night his body gave out, the doctors ordered exploratory surgery, which resulted in him being put on life support and transferred to the intensive care unit. It was almost criminal. He would have passed away naturally, but instead he was forced to live on artificially, with a ventilator tube down his throat, unable to communicate except though his pale blue eyes. The process of his death was delayed and stretched out another twelve days in the ICU. The family came from near and far, and we could hardly bear it, could hardly stand to watch him suffer, with various tubes and probes stuck everywhere. One of the attending physicians called his treatment "brutality," but said there was nothing anyone could do about it. We were all too angry to feel our grief, too frustrated to speak.

My dad, Bob Jay, was a literature major at the University of Michigan before becoming an attorney, so Salinger and Shakespeare were on the bookshelf when I was growing up, and I developed an early love of books. But by the time I was old enough to share that interest with him, Dad was buried up to his neck in the abstract and title insurance business he'd built with my grandfather. Between ten-hour workdays and helping the various kids with their homework, he had no time for poetry. Or rather, that love moved into a new sphere.

I remember Dad teaching my brother Tom and me how to pray when I was about four. Every night before bed, he would come into our room and spend a little time with us, sitting on the side of one of our beds and talking through the proceedings of our little lives. Then he would kneel with us at the side of the bed, make the sign of the cross, and recite the Our Father, the Hail Mary, and the terrifying little prayer:

> *Now I lay me down to sleep,*
> *I pray the Lord my soul to keep.*
> *If I should die before I wake,*
> *I pray the Lord my soul to take.*

Like many people, I wondered about the mystery of this prayer—that I could somehow die before waking, that my soul could be abandoned, that I needed to pray, and so forth. It made me realize that death was close at hand, and it made it hard for me to sleep. I did drift off after a while, of course, but not without a great deal of thinking, which is never a good thing. Many nights, even as a youngster, I stayed awake until I heard my parents go to bed, pondering death and souls and model airplanes.

I remember Dad coming home every night by 6 p.m., greeting us all, kissing my mother, and getting ready for dinner. In many ways, dinner was the major event of the day, both in its making and the ceremony of manners, not to mention the cleanup for seven people. But the endearing thing was my dad's interest in the events of everyone's life, what they thought and what they felt. He helped the younger kids with their homework and made sure everyone got to bed at a reasonable hour.

Dad's concern lost its appeal when I reached my teens and became more rebellious. We had terrible arguments over politics and culture, and other rifts opened up in the family as well. There were difficult years and bad times between him and my mother, but through it all, through the very worst of it, my father's love was the bedrock our family clung to. There were times as a teenager when I hated my father, but I dimly perceived he was something like a saint too. We all knew in our hearts that Dad couldn't have any other life than one devoted to us.

He was in the hospital on the one-year anniversary of my sobriety. None of us knew then that he would be dead a few months later. Still, I was surprised by his statement.

"That's a good start," he said.

What? I thought getting to one year was like climbing Mount Everest, but I didn't say much. He was obviously in a lot of discomfort, and besides, I knew enough to know he was right. I remember his head on the pillow, his wavy dark hair gone gray, his face bloated by steroids, but his smile so generous and warm. He encouraged me to go wherever my dreams took me, and he meant it. Dad didn't care whether I stayed in the family business or not. He wanted to see me soar.

Dad was released from the hospital a week after my anniversary, and though he was weak, he returned to work. We drove together from our home to the big office in Port Huron, about an hour away. He didn't have the strength to come in early, but he stayed the whole day and multitasked like a pro, simultaneously overseeing large commercial deals and answering his employees' most technical questions. His reputation was built on fairness, and he treated everyone he met with generosity, intelligence, and kindness, whether they were a farmhand or a federal judge. Before the leukemia took him down, he rose to become president of the American Land Title Association, a great honor for a small midwestern businessman.

I was in denial of dad's mortality, but I think he knew he wasn't going to make it. We were driving home one day that fall, just leaving Port Huron and getting onto the freeway. Clouds darkened the sky, but the sun peeked underneath the mantle and cast a last glow across the land. Long shadows and magic light embellished the scene, making all the world radiant. As we rounded a sweeping curve of the highway, an expanse of sugar maples was illuminated by the setting sun. They were at the height of their colors, standing out of the twilight like an epiphany.

"It's so beautiful," he said.

The softness of his voice as he slumped in the passenger seat, the knowing in his eyes—there was something happening between us that I wanted to keep forever.

"So beautiful," I said.

He was rapt by the illuminated forest, but looking beyond it, talking about everything at once: the lavish colors of the iridescent leaves, the miracle of my return, the bittersweet journey of his own life, now slipping away, but lasting just long enough. Like the dying leaves before us, the best kept for last, the unaccountable beauty, the sadness, the hard-won joy in his eyes.

Dad was only fifty-eight when he died, a few months after my one-year mark. The death vigil lasted for almost two weeks, and it was confused, as many family members came from far away and then had to leave again when he didn't pass, except for my youngest sister, Amy, who withdrew from college rather than leave him. In the end, though, it was just my mother and me alone at home when the call came about 9 p.m., telling us we had to come back to the hospital at once.

Dad had his own room in the ICU, isolated from the rest of the ward. I hated the ICU like I've hated few things in my life. It seemed like an institutionalized torture chamber where people were not allowed to die, and now all its cruelty was being visited upon my father. What was the use of the ventilator and the IV tubes? They only stopped him from speaking, from having any last words with any of us. He couldn't even write.

When we arrived, Dad was in the same position he'd been in for many days, the bed tilted up and his head propped on a pillow, looking at us with tired eyes. I sensed the smallest thread of relief in his eyes, as his minders couldn't hold him much longer, but also a great sorrow. He didn't want to leave us. We were his whole life, and he'd never wanted anything more than to be with us, to be together, together with his family, the great work of his life on earth.

My mother stood on one side of his bed, holding his hand, and I stood on the other side, holding his other hand. The machines continued their thrumming in the unceasing daylight of the ward. She spoke so tenderly to him, "My dear Bob . . . my dear, sweet Bob . . ." Wiping his forehead, stroking his hand, smoothing his hair, and caring for him in every little way she could.

In Dad's last months, I'd seen them together as though they were newlyweds, so much in love and devoted to one another. They had come through the great battles of raising five children, five adolescents, and five young adults. Now, their love was complete, and though they wouldn't get their just reward of golden years together, they wasted nothing in the end. Before Dad's last illness, when he was still confined to a regular hospital room, Mom would bring in special treats, so they could have a civilized dinner together and laugh about old times. They were veterans.

But now was the end of time, the last moments of his life on earth. As we stood on either side of the bed, holding his hands, I wanted nothing more than for him to break the hold of the machines and escape the hellish ward. But I was still too fragile in my emotions to speak from my heart. I regretted it years later, that I couldn't say "I love you" at my father's deathbed, but only murmured again and again, "We love you"—a step removed. It was comfortable to say "we," to take cover in the family, but I couldn't step forward and say "I," to say "I love you." There would never be another chance in life, and I knew it and reproached myself for it as I stood by his deathbed.

Then, a revelation. I could see it in his eyes, the joy. He was looking into something so beautiful, just beyond us, but clearly in sight. Then he was standing behind me, which was impossible. I was holding his hand, looking at his dear face, and I felt him standing right behind me. I don't mean I imagined it; I mean I had the same familiar feeling anyone would have if another person came and stood behind them. I could sense that he was leaving his body but hadn't yet left us completely, that he was free from all pain and standing with us, even as his vital signs trailed off on the monitor.

My perception of his death spun 180 degrees, because I could see that everything was wonderful for him now. He wasn't just released from the torture of the ICU, he was moving into another world. I could see it in his eyes; he was looking into a place that was glorious. I could almost see it myself by the reflection in his eyes, the great illumination. Yet he was also standing behind me, and I even turned around to look. He was in two places at once—or maybe three.

His death now seemed a fiction, that we had the wrong notion of death. I could see the glory in his eyes, the abyss turning into light. In my astonishment, I nearly laughed out loud, laughed in surprise and laughed for joy. He was fully in the light and we were in the dark. He was going to a new world and we were stuck on earth, and I immediately and forever saw death differently. What great fools we are, believing that death is a terrible thing, though surely it is for the ones left behind. But not for the dying. For the one leaving this earth, death is liberation, a glad awakening from a confusing dream. It was clear to me that there is no death, and that my father was now more alive than he'd ever been. I felt him with me for a few seconds, showing me the way I could go one day—his last great lesson.

Now I understood the beauty of the autumn leaves, their exquisite death and their transformation into new life. For the briefest moment, I almost understood the mystery, but it slipped away like a dream, leaving only a fractured memory.

And then the machines flatlined, the nurse turned off the ventilator, and they said he was gone. Dad's eyes never did close, so I tried to reach out and shut them like they do in the movies. Much to my surprise, I couldn't manage to close his eyelids. The nurse told me it wasn't like that, and then did the job properly. This jarring moment and my inability to do a seemingly simple thing brought me crashing back to earth.

Ultimately, Mom and I left to go home through the cold January night, so we could start making calls to all the family. A blessed cushion of time filled the car ride back, in the long-gone way of life before cell phones. A time for silence and gentle words, a time to begin adjusting to a life without him. Once we got back, there were breathing spaces between the phone calls, too, where we could begin to feel the sea change, and we took it moment by moment.

We sat at the kitchen table drinking coffee and eating cookies until all the calls were made. It was a special time together, and I thanked God I was home and sober and not lost on the street in some far-off city. I was grateful to be able to help with the small tasks at hand, to be available once more. Amy had been out for the night, taking a well-deserved break, but she broke into tears when she saw us with the phone at the kitchen table. So many waves of sorrow would come, so far beyond any horizon we could see.

I was the last to go to bed, pausing in each room downstairs to turn out the lights. There was a pristine quiet in the house, like a midnight snowfall, dense with his absence. I moved from one room to the next, turning out the lights in the den, the kitchen, and the hallway, hoping to sense his presence once more. But there was nothing left of our father— no laughter, no arguments, no song. Just his tender love, falling down on us forevermore.

CHAPTER 15

My Brother Greg

Lifeboat was looking good. After five hours' work on deck, I finally had things just the way I wanted them, and I was confident the boat could survive anything now that it was hove-to properly. I sat in the cockpit for the first time since breakfast and looked over my storm-tossed kingdom with quiet satisfaction. I wasn't getting anywhere because of the contrary current of the Gulf Stream, but I was secure.

What was that? I hadn't been sitting more than a few minutes when I noticed the change. First I turned my face to the wind to gauge it; then I stood up to get a better feel. The wind speed was dropping, ever so slightly. It was still blowing hard, but it was dropping from a whole gale, to a storm that I could sail in.

So much for weathering the night; I needed to get moving again. The wind was also swinging to the northwest, so I'd need to reset the sails and plot a new course. Being an optimist, I shook out all the reefs of the main-sail and raised it to its full height. The boat was soon sailing very fast, as the big main caught the full force of the wind off the aft quarter.

If Boreas was the god of winter, then he was on a rampage. The wind was blowing against the current of the Gulf Stream too, so the waves were getting bigger all the time. But *Lifeboat* was in her element, and, despite her age, she pounded through the white-capped hills like a wild horse, eager for the challenge.

There was a danger the mainsail could be backwinded coming off a wave and violently jibe the boat, especially if something went wrong with the self-steering when I was down below. So I rigged a line called a preventer to hold the boom and the mainsail firmly in place. I didn't want a repeat of the first night, when the thrashing of the main almost broke the mast.

It was a beautiful thing to have *Lifeboat* sailing so fast through nasty weather, defying the storm by harnessing its power. But there was a touch of madness in it too, like sliding down a mountain path in smooth-soled shoes. Sailing fast over the hills and valleys was thrilling, as long as nothing went wrong.

As the afternoon faded, my little dinghy was having a tough time, surfing wildly behind the boat. The big swells made it worse, too, and the little guy buried its bow in one of the waves. My heart stopped for a second, but the little dink popped back up and kept tearing along. The dinghy was taking on water, though, so it wasn't riding so lightly atop the waves. The rain had already dumped a few inches in it, and I was concerned about the added weight. Ten minutes later, the dink took another dive, plowing into the face of a wave, nearly drowning in the water, but popping out the other side to ride again. I could see it was getting heavy.

I thought about trying to reel it in and somehow empty the water or get it up on deck. But how could I possibly lift a dinghy that had a hundred gallons of water in it? I couldn't get down in it and bail, because if we hit a wave and the painter broke, I'd be stranded in the dinghy and *Lifeboat* would sail on without me. Besides, the dinghy would be far too unstable to jump into at this speed, and I'd probably kill myself in the process. All I could do was watch and hope.

Maybe the water in the dinghy would make it more stable, I rationalized, even as I watched her take another dive. It wasn't looking good. The little dink was now almost full of water and only staying afloat because of its unsinkable hollow-bodied design. It looked so brave out there in the storm, so full of heart, and I wanted to help.

Then the dinghy submarined, diving under the water and staying there. *Lifeboat* was flying, but the dinghy acted like a sea anchor and cut her speed in half. The poor little dink was under water, attached by a line, but trying to swim and straining the painter to the breaking point. I stood watching powerlessly as my little dink dove and dove to its death. The painter was strong, and it must have taken a thousand pounds of pressure to break it, but break it did with the report of a small-caliber rifle, and the dinghy was gone forever.

I kept looking aft over the waves, and I believe I saw it surface again, far away in the fading light. I hoped it might find a new home one day. Maybe the Gulf Stream would carry it north to the Grand Banks, then veer east and drift below Greenland and Iceland, and finally reach the British Isles.

I couldn't shake my sense of negligence and guilt over the loss of the dinghy. I should've known better, should've done more. It was like losing my brother Greg, on a much smaller scale, but I banished that thought immediately.

There were other problems to consider. The bilge pump wasn't working, and although I wasn't shipping much water, it was a worry. The lights seemed weaker, too, and I wondered what was draining my electric power. I had strong batteries that were charged off the engine, which I ran every day for fifteen to twenty minutes, just to keep them topped off. But I'd had a hard time starting the engine that day, and I didn't know why. Not that it was unusual to have engine problems.

At least the wind was cooperating, after a fashion. It was blowing like the devil, but it was blowing in the right direction. It was a wild ride with the big main up, careening over the top of a wave and rushing headlong for the trough. Darkness was falling and soon I couldn't see the waves, but only feel them. Every once in a while, a rogue wave would hit the boat crosswise and knock us off kilter, threatening to backwind the main. But we always recovered and sailed on.

In the darkness, I felt more vulnerable, because I couldn't see what was coming. In the light, I could get my bearings. I was part of the world, part of the universe, part of the evolution of creation. In the dark, I was in my head all the time and subject to the mad ramblings of my brain.

Why couldn't I see the danger to the little dinghy before leaving shore? Why hadn't I taken action? Why was I so inept? These and other cheery thoughts weighed on my mind as I made a soggy dinner. I hadn't been able to save Greg, I hadn't been able to save my marriage to M—, and now I couldn't even save my little dinghy. And if anything happened to *Lifeboat*, that little dink had been my last hope.

Of the five children born to my parents, Greg had been the star. He was the youngest of the boys and the second youngest of all the children— a bright, funny, athletic, and handsome kid who cruised through the University of Michigan and moved out to San Diego with a business degree. He loved beach volleyball, card games with friends, and mathematics. He didn't drink or drug or otherwise screw himself up—he wasn't just book smart.

But he had a dark side too, and it was deeper than we knew. In those moments, he could be unforgiving and cruel, but he never seemed to stay that way for long. He was more likely to go in the other direction, with a brainstorm that led to the beach or a camping trip. Greg was over six feet tall, slim, and muscular, with brown wavy hair and a magician's blue eyes. He was unfailingly polite with strangers, always ready to help, and generous with everyone—except himself.

When he turned on himself, the world imploded and there were no satisfactory solutions. His thoughts spiraled down with mathematical precision, like the number pi—irrational, essential, and forever unresolved. Computers can calculate pi to a trillion decimals without a conclusion, and in the same way Greg descended into problems no formula could solve.

I was working as a counselor at Sacred Heart when I got Greg's suicide letter, at the same time as everyone else in the family. It was October 1987, so we weren't on email and even long-distance calls were a luxury, as they were charged by the minute. So Greg used the post office to mail his letter, which cataloged the reasons for his suicide over seven manic pages. I could hardly breathe as I read the thing, my hands shaking and my anger rising.

The letter announced that he was a failure in his life, that he didn't believe in anything, and so it was time to exit the stage and quit taking up space on the planet. It was guilt married to grandiosity, and I was ready to kill him. He had never talked about suicide and had never given any weight to his occasional funks. Where was this madness coming from? We all started calling each other, trying to generate a plan.

As we compared notes, the whole thing became more infuriating. Greg had made a point of getting together with the people closest to him in California over the preceding few weeks. With one he'd go to the beach, with another to dinner or a movie, and always capped off by a great conversation. He basically had a good-bye meeting with each and every one of them, without letting on that it would be their last time together. Then, in his letter, he announced that there were a couple more things he wanted to do before he died—visiting Yosemite and other scenic locations, rereading a couple favorite books, and other nonsense. He stated flatly that he would kill himself in a couple of weeks, and that no one should bother trying to find him, as he'd be all but invisible in his old car traveling through California, Arizona, and Nevada, living off nothing but cash.

Greg was the good kid, the dependable kid, the one who finished everything he started—all of which made his letter terrifying, as we knew he would do exactly what he said. We talked to private detectives, police, and everyone else we could think of, but no one offered much hope. They would look for him, sure, but living on cash in an anonymous car (which he might trade for another, he was so smart), left little hope of finding him. We were hopeless and angry, unable to rescue our own blood from the depths, unable to even talk with the idiot and shake some sense into him. We were all in suspended animation for days—and then he resurfaced.

He wouldn't tell us where he was and he kept the calls short, but he phoned a few of us, just to talk. He wanted to reassure us that he was fine, that he was doing the right thing and not to worry about him. He called me twice during the two-week nightmare. The first was a short call, as I remember. Greg and I were always close, especially after I got into recovery, and many letters flowed between us, month in and month out. He would even send me plain white postcards in between the letters— a precursor to email and text messages, delivered by snail mail at unexpected moments—with random thoughts and observations.

I wanted to keep him on the line, but couldn't. As soon as I turned the conversation to the only thing in the world that mattered, he got off the line, leaving me with a dead phone in my hand and a string of curses on my lips. He wouldn't allow himself to be reached, and he wouldn't talk about his suicide. He just wanted to let me know that he was doing great and not to worry. His plan was set. Greg was only in transmit mode, sending messages as if by smoke signal, with no way to receive anything back from any of us. It really got me, because Greg and I always talked about everything, and when we were together, we often stayed up until four in the morning, drilling down deep into whatever was on our minds. For him to cut me off, to only talk and not listen, was completely outside the bounds of our relationship. Neither of us would ever presume to just talk and not listen to the other. We were brothers and friends, and besides, I was his big brother, so I had the right to physically strangle him if he tried to pull that kind of thing.

But there I was with a dead phone in my hand. He didn't quite hang up on me, but he peremptorily ended the conversation. All I'd said was something along the lines of, "We really need to talk about this, you know. You can always do it later, if you still think it's a good idea." But I never got any further, and I didn't know whether to scream or cry. I swore a lot and kept thinking about how to find him.

Some days later, he called me again. He wouldn't say where he was, but he said he was having a great time, not to worry, and all the same crap. It was getting old. I tried a different tactic with him this time, not broaching his impending suicide, but talking and joking around with him about all the things we always talked about. It was starting to work—I was keeping him on the line and I could tell I was connecting with him. Then he said, "I know what you're doing and I can't talk anymore. This feels too good. I have to go." And he hung up.

I was utterly desolate. At the time I was living with my wife, M—, in a little farmhouse five miles from Sacred Heart's seminary campus. She'd known Greg all through high school and then at the University of Michigan, and had even dated him briefly at one point, so we were both heartbroken. It was a terrible time.

My mother had better luck. She was at her winter home when he called, outside Tucson, with her second husband, Dick Bayer, a retired professor of engineering and all-around outdoorsman. He came from strong German stock and had no understanding of this chaos, but supported my mother as best he could. During the conversation, Greg let it slip that he was in Las Vegas for one last stop, so Mom and Dick drove there and actually met with him. Greg assured Mom he would give up his plan and come home with her. He went back to his hotel room, promising to meet again the next morning, but it never happened.

Greg had a .45-caliber pistol and he shot himself through the heart with surgical precision. The police said he left no last note, but had seated himself on the floor next to the hotel room bed, presumably so the bullet could be safely absorbed as it left his body. His driver's license was laid out neatly on the bed, along with information on how to contact family members.

I got the word about 8 p.m. on October 19 by phone. I'd had little hope, so it didn't come as a surprise, but I was still angry and sad and lost. I couldn't speak or cry and there was no relief.

Things move fast when a long-distance funeral has to be coordinated. Everyone came home to Grosse Pointe, arrangements for the mass were made at St. Paul's church, and Greg's remains were cremated and overnighted to our family home. But would they make it in time? I remember sitting around the kitchen table with the rest of the kids the night before the funeral when the delivery arrived. I held the little brown box in my hand that proclaimed the famous advertising slogan: "FedEx: when it absolutely, positively has to be there overnight."

After the mass, Greg's ashes were interred next to my father's in the church columbarium, just up the hill from Lake St. Clair, which I still visit from time to time. It's been many years now, so the pain is no longer acute, but the reverberations from Greg's suicide blew our family apart in ways great and small, and shot each one of us through the heart more surely than any bullet.

Who knew that people could bleed for years and still have sorrow to spare? Who knew how far the echo of a gunshot could travel? Through years and deaths and marriages, Greg's suicide always loomed above it all, like the Matterhorn above the Alps, distinctive and cold, cleaving the wind and sun in half. How many times we all fell off that mountain, slipping away on smooth-soled shoes.

CHAPTER 16

An Awful Realization

Feelings aren't diminished by time or distance, and dreams are no consolation for regret. As glad as I was to be sailing hard in the right direction, it was impossible to hold off the flood of memories about Greg by thinking about the Caribbean. Maybe it all started when I lost the little dinghy, but I couldn't stop blaming myself for what I'd done and what I'd failed to do.

But I also knew I wouldn't be able to think my way into feeling better. There were things I needed to do if I wanted to get any sleep. The night was dark and loud, and dinner was long over, so I got up and attended to the day's last chores. The mainsheet needed adjusting, and the preventer that counterbalanced it needed to be tightened. Between the two, the boom wouldn't be able to move an inch, which gave me a sense of security.

When everything was shipshape, I went down below and stretched out on the bunk between the leeboard and the wall, snug and secure. It was a wild ride on a wild night, and it felt a little crazy to try to sleep, but this was exactly what I'd prepared for, and I was dog tired to boot.

Finally, things were going according to plan. I was sailing in the right direction at a high rate of speed, and with any luck I would cover eighty nautical miles during the night. At this rate, I could make Florida by Saturday and stock up for my next leg. The halyard was unjammed and running free, the sails were set for maximum power, and the losses of the past were being pushed aside by the demands of the next moment. I missed Greg, but I was on my way, living the life I had imagined. I went to sleep expecting great things.

I awoke about 3 a.m. and went on deck to check the rig. Everything looked fine, but I noticed the wind had shifted a bit, so I set about making a minor course correction. The wind was still blowing like mad, of course, and the waves must've been considerable, although I couldn't see them. I started the routine task of fine-tuning the steering mechanism, when I suddenly lost control of the boat.

Jibe! The boat veered suddenly to port, which backwinded the main, taking the boat even further left, totally off course and sidelong to the waves. The rig was strained to the breaking point, as the preventer was holding the sail firmly in place. The wind was literally trying to sail the boat backward and forward simultaneously.

My hands were on the wheel, trying to get back on course, but because the boat had turned sideways in the troughs of the waves, it had lost its forward momentum and I couldn't turn properly. I struggled to get some headway, but finally abandoned the attempt and jumped up on deck to work the rig.

I knew I needed to get on deck to release the preventer so the mainsail could work normally, though leaving the wheel was also a bad choice. But there was no other way to stop the backwinding, so I started to move, stepping up on the cockpit seat. Just as I did, the preventer broke, with the sound of a gunshot, and the boom came flying across and nearly took my head off.

"Jesus!" I cried.

It was a furious uncontrolled jibe. The force necessary to break that line had to be astronomical, thousands of pounds of force, which instantly caused the boom to crash to the other side of the boat, nearly tearing the mast down in the process. It was horrifying and I remembered my dad's story about a guy almost losing his arm. Fortunately, his mates were there to tie on a tourniquet and save his arm, but all I had were angels (and apparently, some demons). I went back to the wheel and ultimately got us back on course.

The main was now catching wind properly, but the storm jib was backwinded, so each was pulling the mast in a different direction. The boat was twisting itself apart, and I didn't have enough headway to fix it. If I could've just gotten both sails on the same side of the boat by coming about, it would've been fine, but I was stuck. It was a recipe for dismasting, if ever I saw one, and I knew the whole situation could go catastrophic any minute.

I felt like I was starring in a tragic movie about a crazy guy who gets drowned at sea. First, his boat goes into an uncontrolled jibe, then it goes sideways, then the mast comes down, putting a hole in the hull. All these events are beyond his control and in the end he drowns.

I needed to focus. Despite the insanity, I just needed to keep focusing on the next right thing I could do. There was a quiet beauty to it, as well, and a kind of grandeur. There was a different movie playing in real life, where all hell had broken loose but the guy was pulling it back together, by a combination of major and minor miracles. In this movie, the hosts of heaven were in the rigging, and while they wouldn't pull a line, steer the boat, or calm the waves, they somehow calmed his feverish brain just enough to keep him on task. Despite appearances, all was well.

The boat jibed violently again. This time it seemed like the end, and I had a sickening sense of catastrophe in my gut. The crashing sound of the boom was awful, and I was sure the mast would come down. But the crashing sound had an end, thank God, instead of being the beginning of the end, so I had a chance.

I went through another round of acrobatics, jumping from the wheel to the lines and back again. It seemed just bad enough and just crazy enough that I might lose my mind. Resetting sails, hauling lines, releasing lines, and trying to get back to the wheel—I was always three steps behind and increasingly exhausted. At the same time, everything I did seemed to be sabotaged by the power of the storm and the physical abuse of the gale-force winds.

But there was also a calm in the midst of the tempest, a presence. It wasn't a question of belief or faith—I knew based on experience that God was with me, and with me in a way that was physically closer than the storm. I knew this might be the end of my time, but I wasn't fearful. God was closer than death and there was more to come.

Still, the horror of the night and the monotony of the problems nearly overwhelmed me. Everything I did seemed to spawn another complication, and I couldn't maintain control of the boat. Setback followed setback, and I became so discouraged that I nearly collapsed.

I did my best to banish the negative thoughts and keep my hands busy. Focus. The only question was whether the angels were singing a funeral dirge or a psalm from the Divine Office. I felt I wasn't alone, except there was no one to physically help me. I could almost hear the words on the wind: "Even though I walk through the valley of the shadow of death, I will fear no evil."

Well, maybe a little fear. But I worked through one calamity after another until all was ultimately made right in whatever way I could manage, and I sat down to rest. After three-and-a-half hours of chaos, *Lifeboat* and I were sailing straight again. The morning light was curtained off by the clouds, but at least I could see my surroundings again and the pitiless face of the gale.

I finally went down below and tried to get some sleep, but I couldn't stop worrying about the boat. I just didn't trust the rig, so I got out of the bunk, got back on deck, and went to work. The mainsail had to come down, and it took me another hour and a half to drop the sail in the awful wind and furl it to the boom, a job which shouldn't have taken more than fifteen minutes. *Lifeboat* was now sailing on storm jib alone and still sailing fast. There was no danger of jibing and the boat was secure.

Through the morning hours, the wind shifted to the east, bringing waves from the east, which confused the seas. I was too exhausted to care and hardly noticed the increased battering against the hull sides. I needed something to eat, but couldn't muster the energy to cook. Ham and cheese on damp bread seemed like a banquet.

My thoughts were confused too, as I thought back to the aftermath of Greg. As I chewed my sandwich and looked up into the rain, I thought of M—, the lovely girl I'd been married to at the time. After Greg died, things crashed down in the most unexpected way. She was entirely innocent, and the whole mess was unsalvageable. I could hardly bear to think of it, sitting in the rain, and instead said "God damn it," with my mouth full, and tried without success to get her out of my mind.

Greg had introduced me to M— in 1985, a girl he'd dated in high school and had also known at University of Michigan. When we met, she'd just returned from a Peace Corps job in Africa, living in a remote village in Congo. For two years, her greatest luxury had been a leaky tin-roof shack and the occasional daylong trek to a larger village where scraps of the outside world, like a working television, were on display in the general store. She was readjusting to life in the United States, living in a small apartment in Grosse Pointe, and preparing to do some writing.

I remember her trying to explain Congo to me. She told me a story about her small Peace Corps team trying to build a clean water system for a neighboring village: the struggle to get the villagers to understand the need for clean water, the battle to get the elders to allow its construction, the education required to get the villagers to use the latrine downstream of the clean water source (and never above), and the endless weeks of wrangling to get it all accomplished. Six months after completion of the project, she revisited the village, only to find that the system had been demolished and the people had gone back to their old ways, promoting diseases of every sort. When she asked why they'd destroyed the clean water system, she was barraged with accusations, fueled by superstitions and suspicions, blaming the Peace Corps for foisting a strange abomination upon them.

M— had a good and big heart, and between her bouts of malaria and dysentery, the stifling paternalism of village life, and the overall resistance to progress, she came back without sentimentality or hope. It was better, she said, to concentrate on helping people close to home, especially since there was no shortage of need in the U.S. Still, she had an abiding love for the women of the village, who did almost all the work in the fields, the raising of children, the hauling of water, and so forth.

M— was quiet and smart with a head of thick, wavy brown hair of uncertain style and a musical laugh that echoed the innocence of childhood. She was seemingly allergic to makeup and had a pure Irish face that was open and direct. Her eager brown eyes were inquisitive, but also tempered by sorrow. She went to great lengths to conceal her bombshell figure, which only made her more attractive to me. I was living alone at the time in a three-bedroom apartment, playing guitar, running with my sober buddies, and living life full blast. I was still working the office job at that time, but my friends were many, and we were all finishing up our twenties, heading into our thirties, and constantly on the lookout for the Right Person.

Greg was living in San Diego then, and he told me about M—, so I asked her out and things developed quickly. We were head over heels in short order, and we connected on every level. Our relationship was literary and steamy, and she moved in with me a few months later, which put our hormones in high gear and probably sealed the deal. I couldn't get enough of her and she was entirely devoted to me. I wanted to make her happy and soon proposed, scraping up every dollar I could for a nice ring and setting a date for the wedding the following year. We were the coolest couple around, and we played in the garden of new love for quite a while, surfing easily over the ups and downs, building a new life on dreams come true.

After we got married, I quit my dreary job and starting working as a counselor at Sacred Heart, which required us to move to the country, about an hour outside Detroit. We rented an old farmhouse, and she got a job with an environmental group. We enjoyed the land, the simple beauty of the sunsets, and our work, but the isolation was rough and our paltry incomes often left us scrambling to buy groceries. But we knew we were building something good and right, so we got through it all, blessed by the vibrant sexuality that God grants newlyweds. We struggled through the cold winter, the sweltering summer, and our dwindling pennies. M— was working slowly on writing, I was blossoming as a young clinician, and I remember being happy.

Then Greg killed himself, dropping a nuclear bomb into all our lives. Instantly, the landscape changed, becoming poisonous to all living things. The funeral and the constant, grinding regrets were like radioactive waste, invisible and deadly. My questions took a predictable course: What could I have done differently? Why couldn't I save my brother, if I was such a good counselor? I knew he'd had black moments, but who didn't? I knew he couldn't settle on a girl, that his relationships were a little screwy, but he was in his twenties. Why didn't I see his depression?

Greg had written me almost constantly since I'd gotten together with M—, but near the end he asked for a new kind of communication. He was very formal about it. He wanted to be able to discuss certain unnamed subjects without restriction or question, which made no sense to me, since we already talked about everything in the universe. I told him he was crazy and asked him what he was talking about, but he wouldn't tell me. I only found out later.

It happened about two months after Greg's suicide, when M— and I were driving into Grosse Pointe to attend a Christmas party. It was a long drive, and as we were talking, she turned to the history of her relationship with Greg. Her story quickly outstripped the bounds of what I thought I knew about them and swept me into a nightmare.

M— told me that she and Greg had first gotten together in high school, which I knew, but that their relationship had continued on and off with great passion all through college. He'd broken off the relationship several times, but had always come back to her. Even after graduation separated them geographically, he kept renewing the relationship, breaking it off, and coming back to her again. She was understandably frustrated with his constant breakups and wanted to put some distance between them, which made her choice of the Peace Corps all the more attractive. But she literally had to move to another continent, to a place where communication was all but impossible, to finally drive a wedge between them.

Knowing how screwy Greg had been with girls the last few years, I realized that they'd only been placeholders for M—, the love of his life. In his crazy way, he was completely attached to her, even though he was incapable of building a lasting relationship. As her story unfolded, I could feel Greg's obsession, his attempts to control, the great power of his emotions, and I came to an awful realization. He couldn't leave M— and he couldn't build a life without her, so he introduced me to her and hoped I would take her away, which I did. And he absolutely couldn't deal with it.

M— and I had now arrived at the location of the Christmas party, but we were still sitting in the car with the engine running, parked in the dark December cold. There was no way for her to understand the impact of her story, as she thought she was relating things I already knew. Her relationship with Greg had never been a secret, and he and I were so close, there was no reason for her to think I didn't know everything. I later learned that my sisters also knew the history and they assumed I knew it too. But while Greg and M— were going through their tumultuous years, I was deep in my alcoholism and oblivious to Greg's life. He was a confirmed nondrinker, so in those years we had little contact, and when we did get together, he tried in vain to pull me out of the bar and away from the bottle. How would I know or care who he was dating? I didn't give a damn about anybody or anything in my drinking days.

But sitting in the car with M—, I could see how the whole dreadful movie had played out. Greg moved to San Diego, but couldn't get her off his mind. She finally went to Africa, but he still wrote to her. When M— came home, she wisely refused to have anything to do with him romantically, though they would always be friends. There was enough space between them for her to strictly refuse him, and he knew it. So he put me in the picture, told me I should ask her out, and then returned to San Diego. I accomplished the one thing he never could: develop a great, happy, stable relationship with M—. It literally killed him.

I now understood the anguish he couldn't name and couldn't talk about. Now, too late, I saw how my happiness with M— must have driven him mad with grief and self-loathing. But mostly, I saw the corrosive anger he had with himself and his inability to live with the woman he loved. In some ways, I may have been Greg's closest friend, but he couldn't talk to me about these things. He was willing to discuss everything except the one thing that mattered most.

On that dark winter night, M— was entirely unaware of my ignorance. I mumbled something about never knowing, never realizing, but I said little more. We weren't responsible for Greg's death and I knew that, but I saw clearly how I'd played an unwitting role in his emotional downfall, and I cursed myself for my blindness. I could easily imagine how our marriage had exploded in his brain, giving him no way out and driving his insanity.

"I've got to go," I said.

I couldn't go into the Christmas party and started the drive back to our home. I'm sure M— didn't realize that another bomb had just gone off in the car and that her husband was buried under the rubble. I didn't blame M— in the slightest, because she was always honest. But the marriage would be over in less than a year, no matter how we tried to hold it together.

And we did try. We used a small inheritance I'd received from my grandfather to buy a little house in St. Clair, Michigan, and went to work fixing it up. We got counseling and tried to talk about our feelings. But we didn't make much progress, as I had all but decided to leave the marriage, though I didn't admit it, even to myself. As the stress inside the relationship grew, we discovered all the things we didn't have in common. The house grew quiet and cold, and we talked about other people. We uncoupled and started drifting along different currents.

Though I initiated the separation, the divorce was even more painful than Greg's suicide, if only because the process dragged on for so many months. Many times I hoped we might start over. I remember coming to visit M— at the house before the divorce was finalized, praying fervently that we might reconnect. If I could just see her smile again, if I could just see some flicker of willingness to risk everything and try again. But I didn't see it, and I couldn't blame her.

It was an awful time, but the long nightmare gradually ended and morphed into dreams, and the dreams led me out of the darkness. I knew

I had to start over, and this time I'd do it differently. I'd be a dangerous man, as T. E. Lawrence would say, and dream with open eyes—a dreamer of the day.

In the days of my divorce, the dream of boats took hold again, and I began to read everything I could about solo sailing. I read all the greats, beginning with Joshua Slocum, and even bought my Aries from Hal Roth. If those men could do it, I could do it, and so it began. I wanted to start over fresh and sail.

Which was where I now found myself on *Lifeboat*, eating a sandwich in the rain. The cockpit was a grim place that day, with the storm thrashing us nonstop. Had the sun ever shown itself on this godforsaken planet? Would it ever warm my skin again?

There was little to hope for in these conditions; only faith remained: faith in the hull, faith in the rig, and faith in God. I had *Lifeboat* set for storm sailing, and she was doing her best, straining endlessly against the gusts. The bilge pump was out and the engine wouldn't turn over, but I didn't have the energy to troubleshoot either one. A puddle of water was sloshing around in the cabin below, but I'd given up worrying about it. We would either sail through this thing or sink.

But I wasn't all doom and gloom, either. After all, storms rarely last more than a few days, so in all likelihood, the worst was probably just about over. I decided to go down below and take a nap.

CHAPTER 17

Cannon below Deck

I slept for a couple of dreamless hours, released from every care, inside and out. I awoke in time to catch the last shreds of daylight and my last best chance of the day to assess the storm. There was no improvement.

I tried to turn on the navigation and cabin lights, but everything was dead. What had drained away all my power? The question plagued me, but there was no way to troubleshoot the electrical system now. Something had probably shorted out in the flooded bilge and depleted my batteries, so I had no juice, no engine, no compass light, no nothing. I dreaded the blackness of the night and the vulnerability of blindness. I still had a few precious flashlight batteries left and the decorative kerosene lamp affixed to the cabin bulkhead. Thank God the old thing actually worked.

Daylight vanished early, and my visible world shrank down to the confines of the boat, with all my foreboding projected out on the darkness. I'd lost control of the boat so many times now and the wind was blowing so hard that it seemed foolhardy to begin the long night rushing full speed through the gale, even if it was in the right direction.

Lifeboat was running at seven knots under storm jib alone—very fast for a sailboat—and it just seemed too much, especially if I had another problem with the steering gear. The boat felt like a runaway train, zooming down the mountain with no brakes, destined for a terrible crash. Even though I was finally making good time in the right direction, I decided the boat needed to be hove to for the night, so we could ride the storm more easily. This strategy would stop my forward progress, it's true, but making time was no longer my first priority.

Since the mainsail was already down and furled to the boom, all I had to do was back the storm jib to the wind and adjust the rudder hard over. The result would be that the sail would push the boat off the wind and the rudder would steer into it, causing a gentle back-and-forth motion.

The job should've only taken ten minutes to complete, but nothing was that easy on *Lifeboat*. As I loosened the jib sheet, the sail bucked and the sheet attached to it jumped, catching itself in the foredeck hatch and sticking fast. The problem was serious, so I had to get up on the foredeck right away. It was already dark, so I grabbed the flashlight, clipped my safety harness to a line I'd rigged from bow to stern, and ventured out.

Though it was only forty feet from the stern rail to the bow pulpit, clambering out on the deck in the dark seemed like a major expedition. The deck was awash with spume and rain, pitching up, down, and sideways, and the dim circle of my flashlight was the only light I could see.

Walking upright was impossible, but crawling wasn't a great option either, so I half-squatted and hunched over like an old-time coal miner trying to crab his way to the coalface. The "one hand for yourself, one for the ship" rule meant I needed to hold on to something that wouldn't move, and then use the other hand to do whatever work was required. In practice, this was impossible, since I needed the other hand to hold the flashlight. So I kept one hand on the boat and one on the flashlight, until I actually had to do something, and then I just did the best I could.

Scrambling up on deck was dangerous, but I was exhilarated too, in the baffling way that men and boys are driven to do crazy-ass things. As I started out from the cockpit, I was grinning like a fool, intent on stealing a prize from the cookie jar of fate. I had to free that snagged line, and I loved the fact that I was literally facing hell and high water. As I got on deck, they both seemed to be licking their chops, so I stayed low, holding onto the teak handrail that ran along the side of the cabin top. With the flashlight in my free hand, I tried to look ahead, but all I saw was the rain blown sideways and the plunging bow.

I took the deck in small steps, to keep my balance. The boat was falling from the crests of the larger waves rather sharply and not just sliding down from the peaks to the troughs. *Lifeboat* was heeled over considerably too, with the low side often slipping below the surface of the boiling sea.

When I reached the end of the handrail, the next test was to make it to the mast, only a few feet away. There was no decent handhold between my position and the goal, so I squatted there to plot my next move. The boat slammed into a big wave and shuddered, the deck buried in seawater. The last of the wave pulled at my sea boots as it receded, hinting at its real intentions, but gently, like a beach wave sucking sand around suntanned feet.

I had to pick my moment and go for it. I waited for a deep trough in the waves and then took three quick steps to the mast, keeping my center of gravity low. It seemed easy enough, but I slipped slightly on the last step and slammed my kneecap into a low brass winch on the mast. The pain was quick and deep, and I gripped a halyard tightly and tried to bend my right leg.

The deck was awash again, but I couldn't put any weight on my right foot yet, so I leaned against the mast and clung to the halyard. "Son of a bitch," I said to the storm. The pain radiating from my knee was considerable. I wasn't grinning anymore and wasn't so excited to be out on the foredeck, but I was more determined than ever. The damned knee hurt like hell.

I switched on the flashlight and tried to assess the state of the lines. I had things relatively shipshape, with all unnecessary clutter cleared from the foredeck. Only the minimum remained, so it was easy to see the source of my trouble: the jib sheet was caught on the foredeck hatch. The stupid thing. Why did it have to go and snag itself? I balanced on one leg, flexed my knee, and wondered how I was going to go the next ten feet.

I couldn't do my low crouch walk anymore, so I eased myself down facing backward, put my butt on the deck, and started pulling myself along the high side. Gravity wanted to yank me down to the low side, aided by the slippery deck, but I pulled myself along the lifelines toward the hatch.

Another big wave washed over the deck, lifted me slightly, and set me back down, the backwash finding its way up the leg of my foul-weather gear and down into my boot. I kept moving forward, muttering something ugly and dragging my butt along the deck.

The foredeck hatch was a heavy, wood-framed square with a thick, frosted polymer top to let in light. It was hinged on the backside to allow access to the V-berth below, and it was big enough for a man to crawl through. Its wooden frame needed repair, because the fingers of the joints at the corners were starting to separate with age, making a good catch for the line. It seemed about half an inch of one corner of the hatch was sticking out just enough to snag the braid perfectly. I was on top of it now.

I couldn't just flick it free, though, as the full force of the sail had set it in place. I pulled myself a bit farther out toward the bow, got a better angle on it, and yanked it out. Pulling myself back a few feet, I made sure the line ran free and wouldn't snag again. I didn't want to stay out there long, because if the boat plowed into a big wave, I could be carried off the bow in a wink.

I used the flashlight to check around, and all the other lines looked good, so I started crabbing my way back toward the cockpit. I decided to test my knee again and used the mast to shimmy my way to my feet. The knee wasn't too bad now, so I hobbled back to the cockpit the same way I'd come, keeping a firm hand on the cabin handrail.

I was surprised how unmanageable the boat was feeling, as though she might turn turtle and swamp in one of the big waves. *Lifeboat* should've been riding much easier, but instead she felt unsteady. My heart sank as I realized that the storm was gaining strength. The shrieking of the wind was getting louder and the pitch was getting higher. Even being hove to under storm jib wasn't enough to ride it out.

Then I heard a loud explosive sound, like a cannon going off below-decks. Had the hull cracked? Was the boat sinking? My heart was in my mouth as I raced down the companionway steps to look for flooding.

The same old puddle was sloshing around on the sole of the cabin, and I thought it was getting bigger. But was it? I stared at the water for several minutes, until I was convinced there was no danger. I wasn't sinking at the moment. But whatever that sound was, it wasn't good.

The situation wasn't safe, period. I'd been foolhardy to go out so far alone in a boat set up for a racing crew, and now I was in trouble. My faith in the old boat and my ability to manage it was gone. The idea of getting on the radio and calling for help was too embarrassing to contemplate, but anyone could see things were deteriorating. My radio could work on low power, and I knew the Coast Guard had the ability to pick up very faint signals. I hated to admit it, but I needed to call for help.

Around 8:30 p.m., I picked up the corded mike on the marine radio and turned it on. I couldn't wait until the boat was actually sinking—there wouldn't be time—I needed assistance now. But the radio wouldn't turn on. There was no static, no power light, and no display on the channel selection screen. I stood in the small puddle at the foot of the companion-way steps, looking quizzically at the dead mike in my hand. Apparently, my two large marine batteries didn't have enough juice left to power a lousy one-watt distress call. Had I purchased a handheld marine radio for backup? No.

The sense of isolation I felt was vast, stretching out beyond the horizon of time. I had always been alone out here, but the chance for help from a nearby ship or the Coast Guard had been a given. With my radio dead, it might as well have been 1492. My isolation was now complete, but I couldn't afford the luxury of despair. The situation wasn't necessarily dire, so I shut down my worst-case-scenario thinking and turned my attention elsewhere. I rechecked the lines and verified that *Lifeboat* was hove-to properly. Everything was battened down tight, and, barring an unforeseen collision or calamity, *Lifeboat* and I would be fine.

Then, another explosion. It sounded like the boat was breaking apart, like the hull had cracked. I checked the cabin and the puddle down below, but couldn't find any leak. I'd never heard such a sound on a boat, ever, and I strained to understand what was going on.

I finally determined that with only a headsail, my rig was unbalanced and twisting the deck against the hull like the lid on a shoebox. The bulkheads that gave the hull its strength and separated the boat into cabins were flexing against the sides of the hull. These bulkheads were supposed to be fixed in place, but the twisting deck was shifting them with tremendous force, sounding like a cannon going off inside the cabin. The now-random blasts, coming out of nowhere, scared the bejeezus out of me every time.

By 10 p.m., the darkness seemed to have been cloaking me for days, not hours. I'd lit the kerosene lamp, which made the cabin mildly smoky, and the cockpit was scoured with seawater and rain. I used all my senses to discern any slackening in the wind or waves, but just the opposite seemed to happen, as the gale piped up another notch. The damned thing just wouldn't leave me alone, and my dead reckoning showed that I was losing my previous gains.

The bulkheads were exploding against the hull sides every five or ten minutes. It sounded like a hull breach every time, and I realized that I wouldn't know the difference until there was a foot of water in the cabin. If there were a real breach, the rushing water would fill the boat faster than a fire hose.

And it wasn't just the bulkheads I was worried about, either. When I bought *Lifeboat*, I'd had a marine surveyor go over every inch of it with me. At one point, he removed a section of the cabin floor to show me the steel plating where the keel was attached to the hull. It was badly corroded, and it was obvious that several of the keel bolts needed to be replaced. It would be a colossal job, but he said I didn't need to worry about it immediately, as long as I monitored any leaks and took it easy.

The ten-thousand-pound lead keel wasn't going to fall off, but it could start to work itself loose just enough to open a gap where water could get in. Normally, the bilge pump would be able to handle minor leaks, but I had no working bilge pump anymore. And how would a loosened keel impact the integrity of the hull? These kinds of problems were all manageable on a day sail, as one could always return to the marina and haul the boat out of the water on a big hoist for inspection.

Maybe it wasn't the bulkheads, after all. Were the explosive cracking sounds coming from another source? I didn't want to speculate, but I was aware of the likely consequences: the boat would sink and take me along with it. It seemed like the wind was screaming at me just to make a point. The most likely scenario in the next eight hours was catastrophic. One thing had led to another, and there were zero rescue options. The old boat couldn't take the constant punishment of the storm and I had no life raft. I'd read about this kind of thing plenty of times, but I'd rationalized it would never happen to me. The storm's colossal strength was proving otherwise, and I was waking up to the facts much too late.

I tried not to think about it, because if the boat were to sink, there would be almost nothing for me to do. I already had a life preserver on, but it wouldn't do me much good, especially with all the clothes and foul-weather gear. I could see myself flogging in the ocean waves, trying to get the foul-weather gear off before it filled with water and pulled me under. Would this night be my last? I could almost hear a small cry within me, like a distant bell tolling the hours.

Was this it? One more booming report from the bulkheads and down we go? I could feel every bolt and stay overextended, groaning and cracking under the strain. Would it all end here? Was this why I got sober? The last question was a nosedive into self-pity, and I wasn't going to allow myself to fall into that trap.

I just didn't want it to hurt. I didn't want to flail around in the water for hours, waiting to get exhausted and drown. If I had to die, I wanted it to be quick. With all the fury of the wind and the booming sound of the bulkheads, I got quiet inside and started talking to God.

I don't want to suffer. Forgive me my sins, and let it be over quickly.

CHAPTER 18

Last Supper

There was water sloshing on the floor and junk strewn everywhere. Books, sailing gear, and miscellaneous junk had been thrown from normally secure drawers and lockers and tossed around the cabin like the remnants of an all-night party. It was a mess, but it was also the least of my worries, so I got myself something to eat. Another cannon report thundered in the cabin, and I thought for sure I was headed to the bottom of the ocean. Maybe it would be better to be trapped in the cabin, as I'd drown sooner, instead of bobbing around in the waves.

My body ached, but I was also pumped with adrenaline, which rose and fell like the sea. How fine it would be to sleep in a warm, dry bed, to stretch out peacefully like the rest of the world was doing that night, whether rich or poor, young or old, good or bad. How very fine it would be, how utterly luxurious to lie down in the solidity of the earth and fall asleep. I could almost remember the feeling of clean sheets and blankets and quiet night air. To think I could've been in bed with my own sweet love, the day's work done, safe and sound and secure.

But instead I was standing in the galley spreading peanut butter on cold bread. I smiled at these fantasies, as though I were examining the artifacts of someone else's past. My home was now a big sailboat in the middle of the ocean, and I was playing the role of captain, crew, and boat knave, crashing madly through the night, as likely to die as to live. And I saw myself for the crazy man that I was, in a bed of my own making, and it was marvelous and sad and frightening. I concentrated on spreading the raspberry jam, indispensable for happiness on such a night, then poured more coffee from the stove-top percolator into my spill-proof mug and moved gingerly over to the dinette for a sit-down dinner.

My happiest moments had been sitting around a booth like this in an all-night restaurant with friends, laughing and talking and being together through all our travails. I used to have many such nights after I'd sobered up, and when I bought *Lifeboat*, I'd especially loved its half-round dinette, where friends could gather and talk in the unrivaled glow of a sailboat saloon. The forward bulkhead had a beautiful teak veneer, and the kerosene lantern on the wall made shadows dance all around. I could barely sit in the damn thing now, with the boat heeled over like a drunk tilting into a fall.

Keeping my seat was a challenge, and I had no one to share the meal with but the ghosts of the dead. My mood deteriorated as I thought about my situation and the past I'd tried to outrun. I was heartily sick of the howling wind, the pounding waves, and the exploding bulkheads. Would this sandwich be my last supper?

After I finished eating, I went back up to the cockpit. The world beyond the boat was invisible to my eyes, but the storm was relentless, carrying on like a brawl of lunatics. I used my flashlight to check the rigging and then went back down below. There was no point in sitting in the outdoor madhouse.

The darkest hours of night are fertile time for circular thoughts and the high church of regret. It's the ideal time for picking over the mistakes of the past and gathering evidence for the court of self-condemnation. I couldn't help but think of my girlfriend Z—, who wanted me so badly and cried so bitterly in the end. No one knew this story, no one in my family and none of my friends; at least no one knew this last terrible part of our ill-fated relationship.

After I'd left M— and been alone for some months, I'd met Z— by chance and we quickly jumped into an affair. My friends didn't approve and implied she wasn't good enough for me, but I didn't care and the two of us dove in deep. Very soon we moved into my old house in St. Clair and settled down to lots of sex, stir-fry cooking, and painting projects. I knew she had designs on my last name.

This lasted for a little more than a year, but the heat inevitably cooled and the time came to split up. It had always been a rebound relationship for me, and I wasn't about to settle down for good. I was going to sail away and remake my life, and I wasn't bringing Z— with me. My plan was for a men's halfway house, for crying out loud, so I couldn't have a girlfriend in tow. I called an end to the relationship, sold the house, and prepared to move full-time onto the boat.

And then Z— got pregnant. She'd been convinced she was infertile, but she got pregnant. I offered to take care of her financially as best I could, but I wasn't about to get married again and I didn't want to play house. She had an abortion, and I've never heard anyone cry the way she did when it was over. She was normally so bright and optimistic, so funny and warm, so dear, but she collapsed as though under the weight of a terrible beating and cried for days without hope of consolation. It was my fault in every way. I knew it then and I knew it sitting in the teeth of the storm on *Lifeboat*.

So here was the karmic result, obviously. And who could question the simple justice of it all? It was perfect gothic symmetry, and I sensed the gargoyles nodding their approval. I looked around at the chaos, at the sloshing water, the mess on the cabin sole, the kerosene smoke blackening the wall and ceiling. The world was going to abort me, and why not?

It was too damn smoky in the saloon, and I got up to turn down the flame, which made it even darker. My unborn child called out against me, against my selfishness and my trifling ambitions. What drove me, after all? My yearning for a calendar picture dream? The pursuit of my own desires? And what the hell were these dreams and desires, exactly? Did I even know?

The irony was that at that moment, all I wanted was a simple bed with a roof over my head. I couldn't ask for more, but I'd thrown it all away with both hands. The list of things I'd ditched was long: running water, hot and cold, indoor plumbing, central heat, and air conditioning; electricity to power computers, appliances, and more; a good car, a good job, a good wife, and all the friends a person had the right to have. All these simple things were the crown jewels of human existence, and I had purposefully and deliberately thrown them all away to be in this hellhole of a boat. Why would death by drowning be anything but my just deserts? I'd earned this fate in the inexorable calculus of fair play.

I was sitting in the cabin with these thoughts, trying to keep my seat in the dinette, which was bucking like a bull. I felt like a criminal who deserved the verdict of the court. The boat and the storm obviously agreed, and they were working collaboratively to mete out the sentence. I was in the crucible now, but soon I would be fish food and the world would be a better place because of it, if the world gave a damn at all.

I decided to put my head out into the storm and see how things looked. It seemed like the end of the world, with waves mounting high around the cockpit, spume blown like cannon fodder, and the incessant shrieking of the gale. A legion of demons followed me back down into the cabin.

Once again I heard the explosive sound of the boat coming apart, reverberating clear through to my bones. Which one of these ear-splitting blasts would be the last? Surely, the boat couldn't make it through the whole night. It was only midnight. The wind was blowing stronger by the hour, there was no mistaking it, and I'd seen firsthand how strong lines can snap like a thread.

I was marooned in the cabin, no longer in control. More regrets crowded in, dominating my brain and overwhelming my heart. How is it that I didn't know Greg's pain? Wasn't I the great counselor? Wasn't I the one the patients loved? They couldn't wait to hear my lectures. "Man, you got that Higher Power!" they'd say. "He's the best counselor I ever had," and all that.

I counted my long hours at Sacred Heart as nothing. I wasn't directly responsible for Greg's suicide, but I was oblivious to the depth of his depression. Why hadn't I gone out to California to find him after I got the suicide letter, even if the odds were ten million to one? What the hell was the matter with me?

The wind was amplifying these charges and wouldn't let up. And the accusations continued. What was the reason for my reticence with my father when he was dying? I held his hand and said, "We love you," unable to say "I." Why had I withheld myself? Where was the "I love you" when it mattered most? What stopped me from committing with all my heart? What was it that always kept me at arm's length?

In my defense, I wanted to hold out my years of sobriety, my fervent prayers, and my service to others. Weren't these proof of my worth?

Not in the least. After all, how much credit did I deserve for doing what was necessary to save my own skin? Did I expect an award for not drinking myself to death? My good works were self-serving.

Perhaps I was a fraud. Yes, I'd managed to dodge the bullet of addiction, mainly because of the unselfish actions of others, but how had I changed? Sure, I was less overtly destructive, less the fool, but I was no saint, and maybe I wasn't even the good guy everyone thought I was. Was the soul of my unborn child here to witness my demise?

Why hadn't I made an effort to get back to church? Why hadn't I tried to find a home for my faith? Hadn't God all but taken me by the hand and led me back from the brink? Hadn't I learned to pray, to make real contact with God *as I understood him?* I read incessantly, talked at meetings, and encouraged others along the way. But where was my commitment?

I hadn't had any terrible experiences with the nuns or priests growing up. Those astonishing women had been my first initiation into progressive thinking and a wider worldview. They were devoted to the poor, and they lived a gospel of love with the invincible power of their vows. What kept me away? I read my various bibles alone. My faith was profound, but I didn't have the protecting structure of a church or the gift of the sacraments. I was just a person alone, pausing outside the door and then rushing off to help someone.

Zen was easier, the Tao was easier, free-form spirituality was easier. Why not go with the flow? I was accepting of everyone and eager to stay up all night to help the next suffering addict. I consigned the church to my childhood and made no effort to discover it as an adult. Many of the intellectual titans of the Western world came out of the church, when it had been the principal engine of academic progress prior to the Enlightenment, and it had produced a number of formidable intellectuals since then. But I'd moved on. My job was to be the catcher in the rye, saving the ones who ran too far off the field.

I wished I'd at least gone to confession; I wished I'd had the humility to ask for forgiveness. I was afraid of running up against an unforgiving priest who would give me a penance I couldn't bear. I just wanted an understanding ear and forgiveness, the kind I tried to give as a counselor. I wanted the grace of absolution. Why hadn't I gone to Quinn or one of the other priests? Why hadn't they ever reached out to me, for God's sake? We were all like statues, frozen in our chosen place. Kindness might thaw that stance, but I wasn't sure I'd find it. Or perhaps I was just too proud. Wasn't that the deadliest of sins?

A terrible crash threw me into the edge of the table, sending loose items flying around the cabin. Was this the one that would send *Lifeboat* and me to the bottom of the sea? I looked at the water sloshing on the floor. Nothing new. The boat must've fallen off a particularly huge wave and crashed down into the trough. She was probably an inch from broaching. But somehow the boat recovered and kept slugging on. I looked again at the cabin floor, expecting to see more seawater, but the sloshing trash heap showed no sign of rising. Lucky me.

CHAPTER 19

A Psalm of David

As the dark hours wore on, I became even more desolate. The boat kept staggering through the waves, seemingly on her last legs, bones creaking, ribs shivering, and ready to crack wide open. The gale was about to become deadly only because of my ignorance and inexperience, and it would soon break the hull, with no way to undo the mess. The sea would swallow me, and my life would be snuffed out just as surely as the kerosene lantern in the saloon.

I was sick of myself and sad too, and these emotions sucked me down into a gravitational black hole until I was crushed under the weight of my own sin. I didn't normally buy into that concept, but in the middle of the night, in the hour of death, intellectual arguments are meaningless. I was a man who repeatedly missed the mark, who in fact didn't have the strength to aim for the mark properly.

I moved around restlessly, sometimes in the cockpit, sometimes in the cabin, trying to get away from my thoughts. I went up topside again and used my flashlight to check the compass in the binnacle and mark my heading. I estimated the wind to be nearing fifty miles per hour, not counting gusts. I made plans on how I would handle wind shifts, and I searched for signs that the storm might be abating, but these fatuous exercises killed only a few minutes at a time, and every time the bulkheads cracked, my adrenaline spiked and my hand gripped whatever thing could steady me.

In these moments of certain death, the concept of sin was rich with meaning, but not of the traditional, churchgoing kind. I wasn't thinking of a transgression or an offense against someone else's rules. The things I'd done over the years were wrong by my own measure, and it was by my own measure that I stood condemned. There was no need for a heavenly judge to punish me; my own mind was perfectly clear and objective. If I had fifty pounds of light in me, buoying me up against the darkness, but a hundred pounds of sludge, then I sank. I didn't need a churchman or a deity to do the math. In the calculus of eternity, I was a seed that hadn't fully sprouted and so I would go to dust, and if I were conscious, this would be a greater hell than Dante's.

Many believe Jesus's sacrifice is the saving grace, but I knew God could see what I saw in my life, and I wasn't sure I'd be saved in a final hallelujah chorus. That kind of salvation seemed unwarranted, unlikely, and, frankly, unjust. I was an also-ran who didn't deserve saving, and I didn't expect God to feel much moved by my circumstances. I'd been given the great gift of life and saved from my own foolishness and foibles plenty of times. If I hadn't been able to do better than this, if I were sinking under the weight of my own defects, so be it. I was about to become human flotsam on the waters of eternity, without even having the comfort of having had children who might do better.

I couldn't see the waves without the flashlight, but I could feel them as the boat rose quickly into the air, up high into the full force of the wind, and then rode down again into the valley, where the spume flew and the waves broke. I was used to the roller coaster by now, but I always had to keep "one hand for the ship" to keep my balance, even sitting down. I tried to convince myself that my odds were decent, but then the bulkheads would explode again, sounding for all the world like the gates of hell blowing open, and I'd be certain of my doom. I decided to go down below.

My mood was black and I reached for the ship's Bibles to wait out my time. It was almost impossible to read, even wedged securely behind the table of the dinette. I had all my foul-weather gear on, dirty yellow and soaking wet, and I sat in the maelstrom of the saloon trying to find comfort with the ancient writers. For me, the Twelve Step groups were where the spiritual rubber met the road, but I wasn't going to die reading AA's

Big Book. Likewise, I wasn't looking for the wisdom of Buddha or Lao-tzu or Native American spirituality. I had a pretty good knowledge of the various sacred books, but I needed to be with the God of my ancestors, the one I'd cried out to in treatment, so many years before.

For the New Testament, I liked the *New Jerusalem Bible*, a seminal translation. I had the heavy, unabridged version in an ivory-colored slip-cover with a Celtic cross on the front. But for the Psalms, the modern translations destroyed the poetry in favor of literalism, which I found intolerably stupid, so I reverted to an older version, where meter, rhyme, and majesty were preserved.

I was glistening with rain and salt water, and the idea of keeping things dry was gone from my mind. I cracked the New Testament first and dipped into parts at random, but I only found the Jesus who was frustrated by the nitwits he'd recruited. Not that he'd made things easy for them. But, like many Bible readers, I didn't think it was chance that brought me to a given passage, so I couldn't help but think he was frustrated with me too. And why not? I'd been delivered from my addiction and placed on a reasonable path to happiness, only to go AWOL and run out into a storm in my own little boat. A nitwit, if there ever was one.

I knew the usual places to find solace, and I turned from the depressing stuff to Jesus's exposition on the lilies of the field and the birds of the air: "Therefore I tell you, do not worry about your life. . . . Can any one of you by worrying add a single hour to your life? . . . Your heavenly father knows what you need."

Kaboom! went the bulkhead, and I glanced down at the cabin sole to see if the water was rising. Not yet. What worried me, though, what was breaking my heart, was the feeling that God knew me and loved me, but that my time had come to be thrown into the fire, like the lilies of the field. It was all well and good to clothe the lilies in raiment finer than Solomon, but they still had to die. There seemed no question that my own time had come and that I had unwittingly chosen the hour myself.

I hadn't been enthusiastic about established conceptions of heaven. I believed the world was a spiritual boot camp and that some will make it to the next level and some won't. The idea of hell only made sense in terms of the place between my ears. There was no need for fiery pits or pitchfork demons. Being cast away in eternity, fully aware of what might have been, was enough to harrow the mind. If the natural world was any example, the universe was a pretty tough place for a soul to get by. There was no way to count the seeds that fell from a big oak tree over time. Tens of thousands, at least, and in the *Tao Te Ching*, ten thousand was the number for infinity. So, tens of thousands of seeds fell every year, and how many became saplings? And how many saplings rose up to be the size and stature of a mature oak? One? Maybe none? These were the inexorable odds of the natural world.

Most living beings, most animals on the earth, were prey. Their lives were more than likely to end in the jaws of another. A fearful end for one, a feast for the other. Sitting in the vortex of the storm, I knew how lucky I'd been to have escaped with my life, to have bloomed and had the chance to grow. Hadn't I walked away from love because I always wanted more? Wasn't my calculus that I could always do better? And wasn't my current death trap the result? I was both predator and prey.

I set down the modern Bible and reached for another translation. This Bible had been a gift from my brother Tom when I completed treatment at Maplegrove. He wrote a memorable inscription, which I paused to read:

> *Welcome back. I knew you'd want to start reading again,*
> *so I thought I'd bring you the book which—despite the*
> *countless times I've rejected it, because through it I see*
> *myself too clearly—is the word of God.*

Tom was a straightforward guy. One year younger than me, he'd taken a completely different path in life, though no less fraught with trials. He was a hardworking father and husband, and he was almost always cheerful and helpful in the way of holy people. Tom wasn't a saint, but I admired the way he sacrificed himself for others quietly.

Now I turned to the Psalms of David. In the interest of time—ka-boom!—I went for the greatest hits, like Psalms 23 and 91. But everything I read seemed like an accusation.

The Lord is my shepherd, I shall not want.

But I'd always wanted more, and now I had it in full measure. The bulkheads were strangely silent at that moment.

He makes me lie down in green pastures; he leads me beside the still waters.

I could hardly read those words and I closed the Bible, leaving the marker in place. I remembered driving home from Sacred Heart through the farmland to my white frame house in St. Clair. I loved my work and was close to all the staff and patients. I was being groomed for the clinical supervisor's job, and I was coming home every day to someone who loved me.

I gripped the table of the dinette to keep from being thrown out of it, as the boat pitched violently in the karmic storm, and waited for the last scene where the bad guy gets his due. The hull made a fearful cracking noise, another cannon shot, and I looked to the puddle to see if the water was rising. But the level remained stable—the remnant of my still waters. I reopened the Bible to the marker and kept reading.

He restores my soul.

This little sentence had always been a breathing point for me, a place where I could exhale and let go of the day. Now, in the hopeless night, I looked off into space and said thanks. Thanks for all that I'd been given. It wasn't gone yet and I was grateful for my life.

He leads me in paths of righteousness, for his name's sake.

It all started when I got down on my knees in the treatment center and called out to Him, even though I didn't believe. My heart knew better and my heart knew His name.

Even though I walk through the valley of the shadow of death, I will fear no evil, for thou art with me.

And in fact I hadn't feared evil since I'd gotten sober, and I didn't even fear death all that much—I just didn't want it to hurt.

Your rod and your staff, they comfort me.

The boat fell off a wave and plummeted down, bringing my heart into my mouth. Once again, I waited for something catastrophic to happen, but *Lifeboat* kept working through the endless sea. In my mind's eye, I could see what was happening on deck, the sail shedding rain, the headstay straining under the force of the sail, the bow sloshing through the hills and valleys.

You prepare a banquet for me in the presence of my enemies. You anoint my head with oil, my cup overflows.

I thought of myself laughing with my buddies in an all-night diner, like men washed up on shore from a shipwreck, laughing ourselves to pieces, so lucky to be alive.

Surely goodness and mercy shall follow me all the days of my life, and I shall live in the house of the Lord forever.

I looked off into space and thought of all the times I'd read that line. What a wonderful exclamation point it was to the poem and how true it had seemed. In my old life, I was always grateful, sometimes inexplicably, just to be traveling through another day.

I looked across the saloon wistfully, staring at nothing, even as the violent motion of the boat tried to throw me from my seat. I kept my left hand free to grip the table, and my feet wedged against the sturdy aluminum pedestal beneath it. I remembered clearly how good it had been to be warm and indoors on a winter night, sitting in my overstuffed leather chair, alone with God.

Psalm 91 came to mind, as I thought of all the people I'd known in my recovery.

A thousand may fall at your side, ten thousand at your right hand, but it will not come near you.

So many people had gone back out; so many had died. I thought of Susie, so bright and funny. She had a young son and worked as a nurse— the very picture of recovery. She moved to another town, not far away, and then relapsed and overdosed and died. So many fell on my right side, so many on my left, but it hadn't come near me. I was safe in the refuge and the fortress—as long as I chose to stay there.

You will not fear the terror of the night . . . nor the pestilence that stalks in darkness. . . .

But the terror and the pestilence were there in the cabin with me, no doubt about it. *Lifeboat* went plowing into another wall of water and shuddered like she might give up the ghost. It seemed like I was being tortured to death, rather than killed outright.

Then I remembered Daniel in the lion's den. He didn't try to fight off the lions; he didn't even look at them. He was completely indifferent to his fate and looked up toward the light instead, and fixed his eyes on God. This was what I'd always done in times of trouble. I'd always relied on my little prayer, "God help me," spoken from the heart.

If you make the Most High your dwelling—even the Lord, who is my refuge—then no harm will befall you, no disaster will come near your tent. For He will command his angels to watch over you, to guard you in all your ways.

This had been my experience in the world. When I put myself in God's hands, there was no disaster. I was lifted out of harm's way and brought through the mess, not necessarily painlessly, but safely. But it was different now, perhaps because I had so single-mindedly designed my own fate, leaving so much pain in my wake. In what seemed like my last moments, my guilt overwhelmed me and I hung my head in sorrow. The rain was blowing in through the companionway like the devil's own breath.

I put my head in my hands and moaned, leaning over the table and the Bible. I could hardly pray, could hardly bring myself to ask for help, but my soul carried on without me. I clenched my stomach and groaned softly. Time stood still in the cabin, and then something inexplicable happened. I was no longer alone.

As I sat at the dinette table, hunched over the Bible, I became aware that someone was sitting next to me—*he* was there in the cabin with me. Jesus was physically sitting next to me at the table with his arm around my shoulder. I felt no shock or wonder at his presence—it seemed perfectly natural. His sudden appearance seemed like a merciful way to finish things off. Who knew what death was supposed to be like, anyway? What had my father seen? I figured I was in the process of finding out.

I didn't even look up but continued to hang my head, accepting my fate. I assumed my death would surely follow, and I waited to see what would happen next. He was dressed in white, but I didn't actually turn to face him, because I couldn't. I was too overwhelmed with guilt to look him in the eye. I continued to look down instead, and I figured it was the end of my run. But I felt a dawning sense of peace too. Not safety from the storm, but rather a deliverance from it. There was no quelling of the wind or waves, but a profound detachment, as if we were already outside of time, even as the crash-bang of the boat continued.

Jesus seemed to be a strong man physically, with an arm that could lift a big anchor as easily as a coffee cup, but he radiated a gentleness that was healing. I realized he was closer to me than my next thought. He knew me more intimately than I knew myself and loved me more than I ever could.

I realized that through the eons he'd known countless living beings with incomprehensible depth—not only the mechanics of their pumping blood and thrashing brains, but all their hopes and fears and lusts and dreams, millisecond by millisecond, through a trillion trillion lifetimes. And all were unconsciously riding on a sea of love and had their very existence in this love. The universe we inhabited was just one expression of this majesty, and it was so vast and complex that it immediately became incomprehensible to me, though I could see it clearly.

I knew that Jesus loved me not in spite of who I was but because of who I was: a child of God. At his level of understanding, my failings were like spray blown off the top of a wave, immediately lost in the vastness of the ocean and returned to its heart. He was there in every synapse—he was in the center of every fear, every joy, every friendship, and every triumph. He suffered through every tragedy, every cruelty, and all despair, as he knew them intimately. And now he was here to shepherd me through my death. It seemed like everything would be all right and that I was already beyond pain.

Then Jesus spoke to me. He spoke warmly but with authority, opening a door I didn't believe was there. His words were simple:

"You can be forgiven."

A great peace settled over my heart. My mind emptied completely and lapsed into a quiet like the mountains. I was in a place of vast tranquility that stretched out beyond the realm of consciousness. I was set apart from the storm and all my fears were gone.

In another moment, I realized Jesus was no longer present, at least physically. He'd departed silently, taking all my sorrows with him. Was this some merciful numbing before death? I didn't know, but I was grateful for it, and I felt perfectly ready to transition out of this world.

I leaned back from the table in amazement, almost unable to comprehend what had happened. I thought I'd probably be with him again in a moment or two. Then I decided to lie down in the berth across the way. I wedged the Bibles in tight between the seat cushions for safekeeping and started working my way out of the dinette. I was so completely flushed with peace, so unutterably calm in my heart and soul, that the gale no longer had meaning. I got out of the dinette, stood in the center of the pitching cabin, and lay down in the adjacent berth.

The wind shrieked as loudly as ever, the bulkheads continued banging, and the boat seemed on the verge of sinking, but none of it had any significance. I laid down fully dressed in my foul-weather gear and luxuriated in the simple comfort of the thin cushion. I was swaddled in grace and unconcerned about what might come next.

I closed my eyes and thought, *Now I lay me down to sleep.* There was no doubt that I was already in God's keep, as I had always been. I wasn't thinking about the storm or the boat or death. I wasn't even thinking about Jesus. I simply lay down smiling in the pilot berth, safe and sound, and went fast asleep. I didn't wake up or move so much as an inch throughout the entire night. I slept dreamlessly, outside of time.

CHAPTER 20

The Second Joy

What? Who woke me? I opened my eyes a crack and saw daylight—which was impossible. I thought I had just lain down a moment ago. I hadn't moved an inch in my bunk. My eyes popped open and my brain exploded. "I'm alive!"

Was I dreaming? For a moment I remained in the pilot berth, looking all around me. I was still dressed in my foul-weather gear, and the cabin was strewn with books, tools, and junk of every description. The storm hadn't slackened, and the drawers and cabinets were thrown open and their contents tossed around like confetti.

But the light! The main hatch was partially open, so I could see out into the gray fury of clouds. The wind was bellowing and *Lifeboat* was still getting beat up by the waves. But I was alive! I was baffled and I looked down the length of my yellow waterproof suit again and clapped my boots, giddy with delight at my good fortune. "Thank you, Jesus," I thought. It seemed I'd been delivered as I slept, as though someone else had taken control of the boat.

I got on my feet and held fast to the galley post and peered up the companionway into the gale. Would this thing ever quit? I slid back the main hatch and started up the stairs into the cockpit. The storm kept screaming its gibberish, but I was so thrilled to be alive, to be quick and not dead, that I laughed in its face and shouted "Hah!" at the top of my lungs, daring the tempest to show me its worst.

If *Lifeboat* could survive such an awful night, I wasn't going to worry about the weather. I knew it was a mystery to be alive, but I also kept turning to practical matters, and I made my mind up to sail hard for Florida. But what a miracle. Every few minutes, I'd catch sight of it again—the visit from Jesus, the words he spoke, the wonder of it all. I could almost still feel his arm around me and the immense ocean of love. It made the Atlantic and this little squall seem insignificant.

The rain had all but stopped, at least for the moment, giving the early light a softness that seemed hopeful. I turned my face into the wind to gauge its strength and convinced myself unscientifically that it had dropped a bit—still strong, but not overpowering. The clouds were different too. Instead of angry gray-black clumps, they were starting to stretch out into more ordinary shapes and looked like they might even break up, though that was probably too much to hope for. The waves were livid and blown with spray and foam, but they seemed a bit less wicked in daylight, bolstering my hope that the wind was abating.

I went to work immediately, stepping up to the cabin top and unfurling the mainsail. There was no reason to remain hove to, and I decided to sail as hard as I could and try to make up for lost time. I was so exhilarated to be alive, so astounded by last night's events, that I seemed to have the energy of three men. I reset the storm jib and then cranked up the rain-soaked mainsail as though it were a little signal flag.

I needed coffee and something to eat, so I went back down into the disaster area of a saloon, lit the alcohol stove, loaded the percolator, and broke some eggs into the skillet. The place was in shambles, with water sloshing on the cabin floor, debris floating in the water, and the whole mass following the crazed motion of the boat. None of this mattered to me, because I was alive and aloft and about to take charge. I gloried in the moment and the simple pleasures of breathing and standing and cooking.

The hot breakfast and coffee were like a Thanksgiving feast, and I sat at the dinette to wolf it down. The Bibles were still stuck between the cushions where I wedged them, and I almost didn't dare touch them, as though they'd somehow become more sacred. I hardly dared to think about the visitation, but my mind couldn't help poring over the details. The boat had appeared to be in its death throes, the bulkheads cracking and the storm howling. In the last moments, I'd been sitting at the dinette, hunched over the table, reading the Psalms and expecting to drown momentarily. I'd been utterly alone with all my regrets, beyond hope.

Then Jesus was in the cabin with his arm around me, like an old friend coming to sit by my deathbed. When he spoke to me, it was like picking up on a conversation we'd been having for years, as good friends do, without any need for preliminaries. I'd been so despondent that I couldn't look him in the eye, couldn't bring myself to face him. Or had I been hallucinating? Had it all been a dream? No, zero chance of that. I had no more been dreaming last night than I was dreaming the coffee cup in my hand. Even questioning the experience seemed sacrilegious.

But my brain wanted to pick over the details. How long had we sat together? It wasn't more than a few minutes, if that. If I didn't look in his face, how could I be sure it was Jesus? Maybe I couldn't prove it, but I had no doubt. Could it have been an angel or some other supernatural messenger? Sure, and if I'd been born in Mumbai, maybe it would've been Krishna. But that wasn't what I'd experienced. I knew what I knew, and besides, what was the difference to an earthbound soul like mine? Wasn't it better to just accept what had been so freely given? Leave it to the brain to screw up a miracle.

But what was the meaning of the statement, "You *can* be forgiven"? Why hadn't he said, "You *are* forgiven"? What was the catch? What was I supposed to do? Or had Jesus forgiven me? I felt he had and I wanted to believe it was true. I finished my breakfast and dismissed the debating team. After all, hadn't I been given the peace that passed all understanding? And hadn't I been delivered through the blackest night? It was time to get on with the work.

The sky was beginning to lighten up and I could detect a loosening in the clouds. Maybe with a little luck I'd see the sun later. In any case, the wind seemed manageable in the light of day, so I decided to strike the storm jib and switch to a larger sail. I didn't give a damn about the gale anymore, and I could always spill a little wind from the sail, if need be.

I strode up to the foredeck, indifferent to the waves. The deck was pitching back and forth, but my legs were fully acclimated, and I took the peaks and valleys in stride. I moved from one handhold to the next like I was moving through a subway car, grabbed the halyard, dropped the sail, and stuffed it down the foredeck hatch. Then I went back to the cockpit and down the steps, grabbed the big sail from the forward cabin, got it up to the cockpit, and carried it forward.

After securing the sail in place, I swung myself out onto the bow pulpit and hanked on the sail. What a glory it was to ride the bow up and down the rollicking mountains of water. Facing backward to address the head-stay, I looked over the entire length of the boat and marveled at my place in the world. What a view I had down the storm-tossed deck, crisscrossed with lines, to the deserted cockpit and the endless seas beyond. I was captain and crew, dreamer and doer, and a freer man than I'd been the day before. Tasks were as difficult as ever, but I felt a quiet mastery over the boat and the storm, and even my own physical body, that allowed me to complete the work more easily. I was sailing in the presence of the Spirit and I felt the power of the salt air, the wind, and the light pulsing through my veins. My heart was strong and my life with God was good.

When I'd had my first transcendent experience in treatment, I was overwhelmed and filled with joy. That first meeting, like the intoxication of romantic love, delivered me into a world I'd never known. It was a vision of eternity, and though I couldn't recreate its full grandeur, the glow stayed alive and guided me into a new way of living. There would be other ethereal moments, but nothing to equal that first joy.

Mountaintop experiences come in many forms, and countless others had had their own awakenings, with their own unique stories to tell. You might hear them at a trailside camp, in a hospital room, or in a church basement meeting. Bill W.'s famous "white light" transcendent event was an important catalyst for AA itself. Most people's spiritual experiences weren't as dramatic as mine, but they could be equally life changing and equally hard to describe. I kept mine under wraps for a good long time.

Weeks, months, and years had passed since that first joy, and the geography of my life had changed drastically, but the memory of that holy hour stayed with me, a living presence. I'd learned to pray from the heart, and I'd found the heaven that was said to be "among you." I wasn't a saint, but at least my eyes were open.

In recent times, and certainly since Greg's death, it often seemed I was in the desert. I still believed, but faith didn't bring its reward as often. Working with other alcoholics helped, but there were often times of sadness, a longing for those who could never come back. I still had moments of communion, but grief was always waiting outside the door.

Now, this second meeting was different. I was no longer a novice, and I was humbled by my own shortcomings. This second joy was deeper because of my time in the desert and my own hard experience. This love was more mature and its fruit was richer, and it filled me with a new freshness and vigor. Riding the bow and fastening the sail, my dexterity was finer, my balance more sure, and my heart was light.

Meditation is often portrayed as a solemn exercise, but out on the bow pulpit, I enjoyed a different kind of solitude—a dashing, dancing, wind-blown reverie. My mind was racing over the events of the night before, the details of the rigging, the new course heading, and a thousand other things. But no matter how fast my mind raced, the Spirit was always there, keeping up with ease and smiling at my work. Silent meditation is good, but physical action in the conscious presence of God is a lofty pleasure.

On that blustery morning, I felt myself living and breathing a sacred spirit, alive in a world where life carried me through the veil of death and into an ever-expanding realm of possibility. The snap shackles still required work to get fastened to the headstay, but I seemed to do it within the beating heart of eternity. Yesterday's storms were over and today's were in full throttle, and I loved them even more for the pain and the joy of overcoming.

When I was done on the bow pulpit, I stepped to the mast and raised the new sail to the sky, then moved to the cockpit to trim the sheets. As the sail filled out and took the wind, I saw it powered by different forces. Instead of regret pushing it from one side and hope pulling from the other, I saw gratitude was the tangible force of will that pushed the sail, and love was the invisible pulling force, vast and incomprehensible. In that gleaming moment, my heart took flight with the sail and sang "thank you" to the heavens.

I went about the other jobs with uncanny ease. The defects in my equipment that usually drove me crazy—the two-man winches, the deficient steering gear, and all the rest—didn't faze me. I whipped the boat into shape and got her up to speed faster than I ever had before. We were flying through the waves now at the maximum hull speed of the boat and heeled over like a calendar photo of defiance.

Back in the cabin, it was time to deal with the sloshing water, the bilge pump, and the mysterious drain on my batteries. I unlatched the companionway steps and lifted them out of the way to reveal the engine, swimming in a pool of seawater. I bailed out the water laboriously, and the source of the problem revealed itself. An old wire had fallen into the water and shorted out at the connector. Though it probably only leaked a trickle of electricity, it had been an effective conduit to the sea, draining away my power over the course of a day or so. Fixing the problem didn't restore the power, but if I were lucky, the batteries would develop a surface charge in a few hours.

It took a long time to set things right, fix the bilge pump, and get the boat shipshape, but I finished all the major jobs by about 2 p.m. and relaxed in the cockpit with a sandwich. I could see the clouds were beginning to break and the storm was definitely weakening. The rain quit for good and the wind may have even dropped below twenty-five knots. Thank God.

I took out the chart to approximate my position by dead reckoning, but having spent so much time hove to in the last twenty-four hours, I couldn't hope to have made any real progress. My probable course looked like drunken circles on the map, and I only hoped I'd done better than my reckoning indicated.

The sun came out for a precious moment or two, spilling gauzy curtains of light on the horizon. It was an exquisite sight, after all these woeful days, and I relished the few winks of sunshine that graced the afternoon.

The wind remained steady and strong, but everything was manageable, and the salt air smelled fresh and clean.

A foreign freighter appeared in the distance, probably six miles away to the east, steaming on a course that would intersect mine in the next thirty minutes. The radio required very little power, and with a little coaxing, I got it to operate. When the freighter came close by, I could see it was an old rust bucket that was lucky to have escaped the scrap works.

I hailed once and hailed twice, and after an absurdly long pause, I heard a heavily accented voice answer my call, nearly buried in static. I asked for current position coordinates, and he replied with latitude and longitude, and asked me what I was doing out here and whether I needed assistance. I told him I was OK, thanked him, and said I was headed to Florida. He made some unintelligible response, as though dismissing a nutcase, and continued on his way.

Back at the chart table, I laid in the coordinates and found that I was worse off than I thought. The position confirmed that I'd spent most of the storm in the strongest part of the Gulf Stream, being pushed north at the maximum rate. I knew my progress had been minimal, but I now found that Florida was farther away than ever, and I threw my pencil down on the chart table in disgust. It was not good news.

Lifeboat was knocking down the miles at a high rate of speed, and I tried to discount the coming darkness. As night fell, I was still without power, though I expected the batteries to build up a better surface charge overnight. The wind was quite strong, and as the world went dark, I wondered about the wisdom of sailing full tilt.

I hadn't expected to see another vessel this far from shore, and I was apprehensive about sleep as the evening wore on. If that freighter had come six hours later, we would've probably collided. If another one came as I slept, there could be trouble. I was headed southwest at seven or eight knots, so the closing speed with another ship would be rapid. But as the blackness descended fully on *Lifeboat,* I saw no sign of lights anywhere and gradually convinced myself that there would be no other ships this far from shore.

Still, I was worried about the rig. Should I put a protective reef in the mainsail and take it easy? Or should I press on to make up for lost time? What if I had another uncontrolled jibe in the middle of the night? Just because the storm had subsided didn't mean there wasn't unknown damage to the rigging or the hull.

I decided to keep the sails up and continue full speed through the night. I scanned the horizon one last time about midnight, searching for distant ships. I remained fully dressed and lay down in the pilot berth with much of my earlier gratitude fractured by the concerns of sailing. It was dark and the boat was flying blind through the night, eighty miles from shore. By any reasonable standard, there should've been a watch on deck, but I was too tired to argue further with myself and decided on at least two hours of sleep. I wasn't expecting any divine intervention that night and hoped I wouldn't have the devil to pay.

CHAPTER 21

Acceptance

I slept in snatches, waking every so often to poke my head through the main hatch and survey the horizon. The rig was holding beautifully, the main and jib straining like a team of horses running downhill, all through the small hours. I couldn't see a thing on the horizon, but also knew that I couldn't see a fog bank in the distance or an occluded running light on a cargo ship. Standing on the companionway steps with my head sticking into the wind, I thought of yesterday's unexpected freighter whose course intersected mine. What were the odds? Apparently, not as great as I'd thought.

Yet when I went back down below and rested in my berth, I had a certain feeling of protection. Even if I couldn't make complete sense of the message "You can be forgiven," I was comforted by the experience and the tidal wave of love that had passed from him to me. I doubted I would ever tell anyone the story, because I didn't want to be branded as a religious fanatic, but it was now an indelible part of my life, a moment when Jesus had come to comfort me. My theological questions were meaningless in light of his great friendship.

I started the coffee before sunrise on my sixth day at sea, optimistic about my chances of making Florida. My position was lousy, according to the freighter captain, but I was confident that I'd made great progress through the night, though the wind had fallen off a bit more. It wasn't until I was halfway through my first cup that I bothered to check the compass. Apparently, the wind had shifted sometime during the night, and the Aries swung with it. So now I was pointing at the Carolinas, and since I was still in the Gulf Stream, I was actually being carried north too. I had been losing ground as I slept.

I quickly adjusted the Aries and changed course, tacking to a favorable direction. But I was getting nowhere. After adjusting the sails and my course, I sat down to a desultory breakfast in the cockpit. How could I have neglected to check my compass heading through the night? Had I really been so distracted by phantom freighters that I forgot this basic task? I hadn't sensed any shifting in the wind, but then I'd been sleeping on and off through the night too. And of course the light in the binnacle was dead, so it wasn't easy to see the compass rose—but it hadn't been impossible, either.

The sun was now making occasional appearances through the breaks in the clouds, and the sea was a steely blue with whitecaps all around. It was the best weather I'd seen in days, and I was grateful for a swift ride.

Then I had a brainstorm. What if I wired my two ship's batteries in series instead of in parallel? What if I combined them into one big battery to increase their power through the line? I might be able to fire up the LORAN and get a fix on my position. It was a novel idea and I'd never heard of anyone doing it before, but it was worth a try.

I went through the contortions necessary to access the batteries, wrenched mightily on the connecting cables, and proceeded with my scheme. I might blow the LORAN to pieces by getting more voltage than I expected, since it was a truly uncontrolled experiment. But I figured the navigational unit was no good to me anyway, so if I broke it trying to get my coordinates, I'd be no worse off than before. Setting down my wrench and wiping the grease from my hands, I faced the LORAN, pressed the power button, and held my breath.

Voilà!

The little screen came to life and the LORAN began its start-up routine. A moment later, I had coordinates: 32.37 north by 77.55 west. It was an impossibly bad position, showing that I'd only made about three hundred miles to the good in six days of sailing, when I should've made two or three times that, at least. Apparently the strength of the Gulf Stream, which I'd never successfully cleared, had kept relentlessly pushing me north, no matter what I thought I was doing, and had done so at a greater rate than I'd calculated. I was a day's sail east of Charleston, and my options were pitiful.

I went back up and sat in the cockpit, discouraged and discontented. My great offshore adventure was a bust. My trip was in shambles, along with my pride, and I wondered what I should do. I remembered being at a meeting once where an older woman had hit me right between the eyes. She was a woman who'd survived terrible losses, but she had sparkling eyes and a great laugh. At the time, I'd been stuck in some dilemma or other and couldn't decide what to do, and we were talking after the meeting. After listening patiently to my story, she lowered the boom.

"God gave us another commandment," she said.

"What's that?"

"Thou shalt not bullshit thyself."

I'd never thought about Charleston, had no charts for that stretch of coastline, and had no way to pay for a marina. South Carolina wasn't part of my plan, and I didn't have time to be straggling into an unknown port five hundred miles from where I belonged. *Lifeboat* was galloping along happily, and the clouds had turned from dull gray to white, but my spirits sank like a rock in the fathomless ocean.

I had enough food and water to keep going for a few days, but I made the decision to head for shore. Most of the inlets along the coast were inaccessible for a deep-keeled boat like mine, and without accurate coastal charts, I couldn't tell where there would be enough water to enter safely. But a major port like Charleston would have plenty of depth and be well marked. It would take me more than a day to make it in to port, and then I'd have to find a place to moor the boat, without the benefit of radio, as the batteries would be truly dead by then. How would I even figure out where to go once I got there?

I was also broke. I'd counted on the allure of Florida to help ramp up the halfway house business on *Lifeboat*, with the attraction of warm weather and tropical breezes. If I could just get one or two paying passengers, my cash flow would turn positive and I could get on with my vision of a new life, floating on crystal clear waters and living the dream.

But it wasn't going to be so easy. Once I got to Charleston, I'd have to find safe anchorage and dig out my leaky inflatable raft to reach the shore. It was dispiriting from every angle, and the more I thought about my uncertain future, the more melancholy I became. The boat was cruising toward the Carolina coast, but I had no more idea of a final destination than I had when I was hitchhiking around the country. I could live for free at the moment, but I'd soon be reentering the kingdom of the dollar with an empty wallet.

God, grant me the serenity to accept the things I cannot change . . .

That was everything, of course: the weather, the Gulf Stream, the foiled plans, everything. But it also meant what people might say, the "I-told-you-so" stuff, the new city, the poverty, and so on. It was all beyond my control.

. . . courage to change the things I can . . .

That was me. I could change my attitude and my actions, and in changing them I could change my world. I had complete control over myself.

. . . and wisdom to know the difference.

I had to remember the last part because I had chronic spiritual dementia. Or maybe it was just that human desires were more powerful than the soul's aspirations. I didn't want to give up my goal, and I didn't want to change my attitude. I wanted to keep sailing south and get to Florida. But I knew my battery gimmick wouldn't last long, and it would be foolhardy to sail in the coastal traffic at night without lights, radio, or navigation. I had to surrender.

A dull sense of disappointment settled in, and I felt I had nothing to look forward to but a cold anchorage and repairs I couldn't afford. On the other hand, I wasn't there yet and I had plenty of issues to consider, like the fact that I had no coastal charts detailed enough to get me safely into port. I had a big chart for long-distance sailing, but nothing that marked the shoals, range lights, and buoys that I needed.

The real trick was to time my arrival for daylight, so I could see where

I was going. For the moment, I had the luxury of knowing my position, and if I could just keep the right speed, I could control the time of my arrival. Once again I cursed my foolishness for not being better prepared. I had control over what charts I bought, for God's sake, and I'd gone on the cheap. So far I'd avoided serious consequences, but would my luck hold?

The wind remained brisk through the afternoon and into the early evening, so I was sailing very fast on a beam reach with the canvas taut and a steep angle to the deck. It was effortless for me now to race up and down the length of the boat, springing off the cockpit coaming, jumping on the cabin roof, striding by the mast, and hanging on the headstay. The boat had become an extension of me, like a musical instrument, and I felt a kind of virtuosity I'd never had in all my years of sailing.

I lingered on the foredeck a while, with *Lifeboat* running toward the sunset, the golden light warm against my face. I had missed my goal by a long shot and didn't know where I'd land, but I was sailing flat out, and I took some pride in getting the Aries to work without having to touch the wheel. So much was going right, even if my dream would be delayed.

There would be no safety tonight as I sailed into the busy coastal traffic, and as the blackness descended, I found my batteries weren't strong enough to power my navigation lights. No other ship would be able to see me, so I took quick naps through the night and kept watch. I spied other ships' lights in the distance several times, but no ship came near me and the wind stayed steady from the south.

A few stars came out, and as I left the warmth of the Gulf Stream, the temperature plunged twenty degrees. It was a long, cold night, and I was eager to find any safe anchorage. I fantasized about sleeping through an entire night in a snug harbor. I lusted for the comfort of a furnace and a meal eaten on a horizontal table. But I knew I wouldn't feel real warmth until Florida.

God, grant me the serenity . . .

CHAPTER 22

Good Samaritans

The batteries gave out for good at about 4 a.m., and with them went the electronic navigation. The last accurate fix I had was about twenty miles from shore and about fifteen miles north of Charleston's harbor entrance. As the morning brightened and I got closer to shore, I sailed into a massive fog bank, a wall of white as high as the sky, illuminated as though from within by diffuse sunlight. Though I was closer to the mainland, I couldn't see more than fifty feet in front of me, so I had no chance to get my bearings. I was completely blind.

How deep was the water here and how much water was under my keel? I had no idea. I tried to reckon my position, but the wind had changed and my course along with it, so I couldn't be sure. I needed a position fix, I needed a radio, and I needed to know where the heck I was, but all I could see were great billows of fog.

As the morning wore on, I took some comfort in the fact that I had to be a few miles from shore and still had plenty of water below me. My offshore chart wasn't good enough to show depths close to shore. Then I noticed a flash in the water. I sprang to the side of the boat, hung my head over the deck, and squinted into the waves. I saw the flash again, not the bottom exactly, but a change in color that signaled the bottom. A change from dark blue to light green in the passing trough of a wave, almost ghostlike, but real and dangerous. My six-foot keel drew too much water to be anywhere near the sight of green water or sand or rock, so I released the Aries, spun the wheel and sent the boat back out to sea. It was a close call.

How could the depth be shoaling this far from shore? I figured I was eight miles out, and certainly no less than five. Was my dead reckoning so far off, so soon? Were there offshore reefs near Charleston? Detailed coastal charts could answer these questions, but I had none, nor any confidence in my true position. After all these days at sea, how humiliating would it be to run aground and sit helplessly without a radio, waiting for someone to find me? Actually, a soft grounding would be the best I could hope for. Countless ships had sunk within sight of land on underwater crags. I still had lots of ways to get in trouble.

The wind swung to the southeast, making it easier to head toward Charleston. After another hour, the fog began to clear, blown out by the freshening breeze. Before long, the wind piped up to fifteen knots or so, and I was sailing hard for my unfamiliar destination. I could finally see the shore, a nondescript lowland area without any discernible features. I knew that Pawleys Island was north of Charleston, but the offshore chart only showed one landmark there and I couldn't locate it. Was I already south of Charleston? Or was I further north than I thought? It was a long afternoon, with the dark clouds coming back in legions and bringing choppy seas with them. My hope of finding a safe harbor by nightfall began to fade.

Oh, me of little faith. Always uncertain, always worried, always rehearsing the worst-case scenarios. I was "all right, right now," but I couldn't accept it. Where was the landmark? Where was the inlet? Where was the anchorage? Thanks, God, for delivering me from the storm, saving my life, and arranging a personal visit from Jesus. But what have you done for me lately?

It wasn't as ungrateful as it sounds. Practicing the presence of God doesn't have any shelf life, in the same way that yesterday's recovery won't keep you sober today. Part of the one-day-at-a-time philosophy was that you had to renew it continually. It didn't matter that I'd been sitting with Jesus in the cabin the other day. The immediate issue was the chartless present, and I couldn't navigate on prayers alone. Could I?

I knew that God was always in the present moment and if I could manage to join him there, I'd be fine. Riding the crest of the moment is where infinity branches off and all the possibilities of the next moment arise. If I could stay there, I had faith that things would be OK.

I was also concerned about the inlet that led to the complex river system of Charleston harbor. It would be easy enough with a working motor, but I had to sail the long entrance singlehanded. The water would be deep enough, but there were two massive rock jetties that stretched out into the ocean, forming a protected channel for the last mile. The wind would be unpredictable, and I'd have to tack back and forth between the jetties where they ran parallel, having no more than a minute or two on any given tack. I could only pray that there wouldn't be many recreational boaters in the channel, not to mention big freighters or navy ships. Things could get ugly fast.

I would have to continually reset the jib, reset the Aries, and trim the sheets. Local knowledge of the waterway would make all this much easier, but I didn't have power, so I couldn't radio for directions, and I didn't have a clue about currents or random sandbars. The prospect was daunting, and if I successfully made it through, my reward would be to enter the confluence of the rivers, which would have their own shoals and hazards, and for which I was completely unprepared. In fact, once I got through the inlet, I didn't even know if I should head left up the Ashley River or right up the Cooper. I was lost even before I got there.

But these future projections weren't helpful, so I came back to the present moment, where I was doing fine. The boat was cruising along smartly, and the rain squalls I saw in the distance hadn't found me. After watching the shore closely, I became convinced I was skirting Sullivan's Island and was within an hour or two of the harbor entrance. The wind was piping up again and the waves along with it, so I adjusted the sails accordingly and settled down for a second lunch, knowing I'd need all my strength to navigate the jetties. Fortunately, the weather was rotten enough to keep the recreational boaters off the water, so I had the approach to myself.

When I got within a mile of the jetties, I saw the unmistakable figure of a sailboat coming out from Charleston. It was only the second sailboat

I'd seen all day, and it was having a pretty rough go, even before reaching the open water. I was moving much quicker than the other boat, which only had one sail up and was undoubtedly using its engine for power. I wondered if I might be able to call out to them over the water. What a lucky break that would be!

If I kept my present course, and they continued all the way to the end of the rock jetties, they might come close enough to hear my shout. I tightened my sails and made all possible speed for the seaward end of the jetties. As I got within a half mile, I could see it was a two-masted ketch with at least four people on board, and I believed I had an excellent chance of intersecting them. Powerboaters are clueless about the needs of deep-keeled sailboats, but this yacht was about the same size as mine, and I knew the captain would instantly understand my dilemma, if only I could reach him.

The sailboat cleared the jetties just as I got within two hundred yards of them. I stepped to the mast, cupped my hands to my mouth, and shouted out as loud as I could. Soon enough, I got their attention and we sailed closer together.

"I have no power and no radio," I called.

"Where you headed?" called the captain.

"Florida," I called. "I've been offshore seven days."

We were getting closer together, and we could hear each other fairly well across the water.

"You've been out in *that?*" he asked.

"Out past the Gulf Stream."

"In all those storms?"

"Just about killed myself," I said.

"Follow me," he said, and turned his boat back around for Charleston.

He'd already had as much of a pleasure cruise as he was going to have for the day, and he took down his sail and motored the rest of the way.

Now came the challenge. I adjusted my course to head between the jetties and prepared myself to run the gauntlet. I'd have to tack like mad to get through the next mile, and if the Aries failed me I'd be grounded or sunk. Thank God there were so few boats out on this lousy afternoon.

The captain of the ketch and his crew eyed me warily from a distance of some fifty yards ahead. With their engine chugging along, they simply drove straight down the channel and headed toward home. But I was leaping around the boat like an acrobat, working the sheets, resetting the Aries, and playing chicken with the jetties. But it was second nature to me now, and I moved from one task to the next with confidence. I knew the music and all the steps to the tune, and I danced with *Lifeboat* down the long hallway of the inlet, seconds from disaster at every turn.

The approach went smoothly for the first half mile, but then the jib sheet caught on the foredeck hatch and I had to run up the deck to free it. There was no time for this little crisis, but I felt almost weightless, flying past the mast, freeing the line, and then sprinting back to my station at the winches. I completed the tack smartly and headed for the next one. The people on the ketch stared and pointed at me with great excitement. I was a star.

After the next tack, I ran up to the mast just to look things over and enjoy the moment. I was truly master of this old boat and felt that all possible calamities were nonexistent as I hung off the shroud and waved to the crew of the ketch. They'd seen me almost lose the boat a couple times already, and I was more than a little proud of the show I was putting on. I just hoped I wouldn't lose it on the next turn.

It took a good twenty-five minutes to navigate the length of the jetties and come into the Charleston harbor entrance and the confluence of the Ashley and Cooper Rivers. I was glad to have a guide to lead the way, and I gratefully followed him past the grand homes that lined the city's shore. He signaled me to anchor near the Coast Guard station and called to say he'd be back with a dinghy to pick me up. The current in the Ashley River can really rip, but it was relatively mild at that moment, so I was able to navigate the small anchorage under sail alone. There was so much work to do with the anchor and the canvas and the lines that I had no sense of relief at my arrival, but only a new set of concerns as to whether the boat would hold with only one hook out.

Soon enough, I heard the sound of a small outboard motor and Lou Hoffman and his son-in-law came out to greet me. I finished the work of closing up the boat, and they questioned me with undisguised awe about being out in the storms. Apparently, it had been pretty bad in Charleston too, although nowhere near as bad as being 100 to 150 miles offshore. Still, they had no experience single-handing a large sailboat and were amazed to hear I'd been all alone for a week. They were knowledgeable about the demands of sailing in general, but they couldn't quite understand how one person would manage it all, twenty-four hours a day. Lou invited me to stay at his house with his wife, Judy, and their family, and I was more than grateful to accept their invitation.

What a delight it was to ride in their little dinghy into City Marina and pull up to the dock of their club. Lou introduced me to everyone, and I garnered instant celebrity as he told them about my adventures. I was a big hit at the club and turned down several invitations to the bar in favor of a hot shower. Armed with a cup of coffee, I headed for the locker room and peeled off my dirty clothes, which were more than a little ripe. Many people know what it's like to walk on solid ground after having been on a boat all day. The sensation of the sea is still palpable, and the ground feels unsteady, as though it were floating on waves.

My equilibrium was liquid as I stepped into the shower. The shower floor bucked and swayed under my feet, and I had to steady myself just to stay upright. But the luxury of the steaming hot water! I couldn't get enough of it and lingered under the fresh, warm stream. No amount of wealth could have provided greater comfort than those moments, and I marveled like an aboriginal at the instant availability of running water. It seemed to me, and still seems to me, to be one of the greatest benefits of the modern world.

Lou and Judy Hoffman treated me like family, letting me stay in their home, feeding me, lending me a car, and introducing me to helpful people around town. My boat was still a disaster, but I pieced things back together little by little and finally restarted my journey south. What would happen then was difficult and miraculous, but those are stories for another time.

The Hoffmans lived in a beautiful old house overlooking the Ashley River, which they'd lovingly restored. Twice. Hurricane Hugo had all but destroyed it just two years previously, but they'd rebuilt and refurbished again, and were now the proud owners of a handsome and historic home.

When dinner was over that first night at the Hoffmans', I wanted nothing more than to sleep, so they showed me to a snug little bedroom at the very top of the house and left me to myself. The ceiling traced the rooflines, with standing height only in the center of the room, and a single bed against the wall. Much to my surprise, when I went to stretch out, I sank down six inches. It was a true featherbed, with crisp linens and a down comforter. I was warm and dry for the first time in weeks. Had the fog bank been just this morning?

One more thing I needed to remember: I needed to call my mother first thing the next day. Long-distance calls were expensive in 1990, but I knew she would be worrying about me, and I needed to let her know I was still alive. Tomorrow would be Christmas Eve after all, and knowing her heart, it was the best present I could give.

Before dropping off to sleep, I thought over the events of the last seven days as though remembering scenes from a movie—from the glowing dolphins to the howling storm to Jesus on the boat. I hadn't come close to my goal, but I'd done something marvelous and something marvelous had happened to me. It would take me years to fully appreciate the journey, but in that featherbed I already had a new joy. I was the richest broke man in Charleston.

I remembered what Mary Butler used to say when a string of coincidences helped turn disaster into triumph, when some glorious serendipity had intervened in a way no one had expected. I could picture her listening to my tale, right down to the featherbed in the upper room. She'd laugh and nod her head, attentive to every word. Then she'd fix me with her sparkling eyes and say, "God can be a real show-off."

Epilogue

Nearly twenty-five years have passed since I sailed *Lifeboat* out into the ocean, and many more adventures followed in its wake—though none were part of the plan. But as I started to write this book, the old questions plagued me.

On the night I thought I was going to die, the worst night of the storm, Jesus put his arm around me and said, "You can be forgiven." I was relieved of all my sorrows and flooded with peace. But when I thought about it later, in the weeks and months and years to come, I was puzzled by his choice of words and a little rankled.

It seemed like he should've said, "You are forgiven." What was the catch? What was I supposed to do? Did I need to repent?

The words *repent* and *repentance* carry a lot of baggage, and they don't accurately translate the biblical word *metanoia*. As early as 150 AD, Tertullian was already saying, "Metanoia is not a confession of sins but a change of mind." People have been grousing about it ever since.

Metanoia in the Bible didn't refer to shame, penitence, or remorse; it was a spiritual call to action. Metanoia meant to change one's heart and mind so fundamentally that the transformation could be seen by others. It meant casting off the old ways and reaching out for grace. Metanoia, the lifting of the spirit to God, was the way out of fear, self-centeredness, and dishonesty. It was a recipe for freedom and a sturdy joy that lasts.

Jesus hadn't told me to repent; he'd told me I could be forgiven, but I couldn't figure out the message. I'd already made all the amends I could, but as I started to write, the question rose up before me like a mountain range before a wagon train. There was just no way around it, and frankly, if I couldn't figure it out, I had no right to tell the story. Understanding the real meaning of metanoia was helpful in some ways, but it didn't quiet my thoughts at 3 a.m.

Then one day, twenty-some years after the fact, the answer came to me. I was driving to the airport through the morning rush hour, and I was making last-minute phone calls when it hit me. Somewhere between the flow of words a sliver of time opened up, and I felt as though I were sitting in a cloistered garden under an old magnolia tree and one of its fragrant blossoms came fluttering down into my lap. And there it was: *I had to forgive myself.*

I was the one holding on to the past, holding on to regret, and flogging myself. I was the one who had to do the forgiving. Jesus didn't need to forgive me, because he'd already done his part. He was trying to tell me that I could be forgiven, if I could forgive myself.

But nothing could be more difficult, because, like most people, I was always much harder on myself than on others—unmerciful in many ways. To truly forgive myself, I had to accept my history and my failings, not to excuse them, but to let them go. I had to find a way.

For me that meant going back to church, but this time as an adult. The example of Pope Francis was a beacon, and the gentleness of Father Bede Louzon opened the way. Relationships demand time, and a relationship with God is no different. I went back to the sacraments, I read new books, and listened to fellow travelers.

I have to admit that I still feel the thorns from time to time. I can't pretend the slate is wiped clean or that all regrets are gone. Forgiveness isn't amnesia. So, I value kindness now more than anything, and I'm keenly aware of our shared journey together and the immense beauty of this place.

Your own journey is continuing too, of course, and so I wish you well. I hope our paths cross again—at least close enough to give me a shout across the water. Remember to "Say Yes to life" and lend a hand—and for God's sake take a risk. You know that journey you have in mind, the big dream that lives in your heart? Don't try to get ready or wait too long. You can always fix what breaks along the way.

Just go!

Acknowledgments

My wife, Debra, is the most generous person I know, except when it comes to my first drafts. She repeatedly said my early work was inadequate, and dismissed my excuses. Her criticism seemed harsh, but because she's such a fine writer, I had to listen. She wasn't wrong, and she put everything on the line for my sake, which makes her the best partner a man could have.

Dr. George Mann, founder of The Retreat, urged me to write this book long before I had the nerve to begin. He died before I finished the first draft. I got a lot of early encouragement from Mike Mengden, Rev. John Franklin, Ph.D., and Nancy Solak, the world's most thoughtful proofreader. My sister, Julie Jay, also encouraged me in the later stages, along with my old friend Bill Redle. The thriller writer Margie Carroll kept me from losing my mind, more than once, and my friend Rod Walczy dug up a wonderful fact that changed the title of one of the chapters (Jimmy C. really had been a boxer).

Spiritual help came from everyone involved at the Capuchin Soup Kitchen in Detroit, especially Brother Ed, who gives so much to so many. I'm also indebted to Fr. Bede Louzon, OFM Cap., at the monastery at St. Bonaventure, whose kindness has been a beacon for many souls, including mine. All the brothers and friars there have my undying respect and love.

Many people have no idea how much they helped at critical moments, including the Pulitzer Prize–winning journalist Andrea Elliott, Rabbi Yarden Blumstein of Friendship Circle, and Bishop Thomas Gumbleton. I'm also thankful that a well-known literary agent like Jane Dystel took a chance on me and worked tirelessly to find me a publisher, along with everyone at Dystel & Goderich Literary Management. The beautiful drawings for the inside of the book were done by Steven Gamburd, and the marvelous cover art for the book was produced by the great David Spohn, with art direction by Terri Kinne. Thanks as well to Heather Silsbee, the book's production manager, and Judy Arnstein for a masterful copyedit and excellent suggestions. Also, Joe Jaksha, my publisher, and everyone else at Hazelden who worked so hard to get this book to its readers, including Jody Klescewski, Emily Reller, Jill Grindahl, and Roxanne Vold.

When the time came for the last full rewrite, I went on a brief sabbatical to Beaver Island, Michigan, and would've been all but homeless if Marijean Pike and her husband, Francis, hadn't let me rent their garage apartment overlooking Lake Michigan. It was heaven. Many people helped in that sort of way over the five years I worked on this book, including Carrie Geiger, Perry Gatliff, Phil Becker, Steve Brunetti, Donna Kirk, Elin Chambers, John Mishler, all the guys at the St. Al's Men's Meeting downtown, as well as my dear friends Philippe and Marta Malouf, who have always believed in me.

One of the most voracious readers I know is my mother, Sara Critton Jay, so her compliments and encouragement in the middle and late stages were more than just heartwarming. She might be the funniest, smartest, and most insightful person I've ever known. There is nothing on earth more powerful than the prayers of a mother.

I'm especially grateful to my editor, Sid Farrar, who believed in the book when others turned away. His gentle guidance was always right on target. Finally, my assistant, Angelica Stokes, deserves special mention. She has read every word of every rewrite for the last four-and-a-half years, and knows the struggle of this book more than any other person. Besides being a deft proofreader, she was always unflagging in her faith and encouragement, and even kicked me out of my own office to go up north and write another draft. I thank God for all of you, and for all the others who fill out the story of the book, especially the late, great Mary Butler.

Glossary of Nautical Terms

Backwind: To direct the wind to the back side of the sail

Beam reach: To sail with the wind perpendicular to the boat's direction

Berth: A bed or bunk on a boat

Bilge: The lowest compartment inside the boat; the engine compartment may be in the bilge

Binnacle: The housing that holds the ship's compass, often on a stand before the wheel

Boom: A large pole perpendicular to the lower part of the mast, which holds the bottom of the mainsail

Bow: The front of the boat

Bow pulpit: A tubular structure that extends the lifelines around the front of the boat, giving the sailor a safe place to leave for changing sails, etc.

Cleat: A device with twin horizontal horns for securely tying lines

Coaming: The raised border around the cockpit, where winches and cleats are also mounted

Cockpit: The outside seating area at the rear of the boat, semiprotected by the coaming and deckhouse

Companionway steps: On *Lifeboat*, the steps leading from the cockpit to the cabin below, which also cover the engine compartment

Compass rose: The face of a compass showing the points of direction, such as north, north-northeast, northeast, east-northeast, east, and so on

Deckhouse: The portion of the boat standing above the line of the deck, also called a cabin or cabin house

Dog down: To secure an object in place with ropes or mechanical devices

Fitting-out: To prepare a boat for sea

Flake a sail: To fold loose sailcloth neatly on the boom, so it can be tied down

Fluke: The part of an anchor that grabs the seabed

Foredeck: The portion of the deck forward of the mast

Foresail: A sail, such as a jib, attached to the forestay at the front of the boat

Forestay: The steel wire line that runs from the top of the mast to the bow; one of several stays that keep the mast in place

Galley: The kitchen area of a sailboat

Gimbal: A device for keeping an item level by allowing it to tilt freely

Halyard: A sturdy line that hoists a sail to the top of the mast

Hank: To attach the heavy brass clips that hold the headsail to the headstay

Hatch: A hinged opening in the deck of a boat, or the cover for such an opening

Headsail: A sail that stands before the mast, attached to a headstay

Headstay: The wire line or stay that runs from the top of the mast to the bow

Heeling: The tilting of a sailboat underway, caused by the force of the wind on the sails

Heave to, or Hove-to: A method for rigging a sailboat to stay pointed into the wind, to minimize forward movement and ride out a storm more easily

Hull: The body of a boat

Jib: A small headsail

Jibe: To turn a sailboat that is running before the wind

Keel: A heavy lead fin attached to the underside of the hull to counterbalance the force of the wind on the sails

Ketch: A type of double-masted sailboat

Knot: A measurement of speed, equal to about 1.15 mph

Lee: The side that is protected or away from the wind

Main hatch: The hatchway opening from the cockpit to the companionway steps and the cabin below

Mainsail: The large triangular sail attached to the mast and the boom

Mainsheet: The line that controls the mainsail

Marlinspike: A tool used in untying knots and making complex rope work

Mast: The large vertical pole that holds up the sails

Midships: The approximate middle or center of the boat

Painter: A short rope or line used to secure or tow a dinghy

Port: The left side of the boat, when facing the bow

Preventer: A line or mechanism that stops the boom from moving

Prop: A propeller

Quay: A dock or wharf

Reef the main: To partially lower the mainsail and tie the loose canvas to the boom

Roller-furling: A modern mechanism for winding the headsail around the forestay

Salon/saloon: The main cabin of a sailboat

Self-tailing winch: A specialized winch that doesn't require a second crewman to hold (or tail) the loose end of the line

Sheave: An enclosed pulley

Sheets: Lines or ropes for controlling sails, etc.

Shoal: A place where water is shallow

Shoaling: Water becoming shallow

Shrouds: The steel wire lines that hold up the mast

Sloop: A single-masted sailboat

Snap shackle: A spring-loaded brass fastening device

Spinnaker: A very large, colorful headsail used on a downwind tack

Spreaders: Rods or struts that hold shrouds away from the mast

Starboard: The right side of the boat, when facing the bow

Stays: The steel wires that hold up the mast and run all the way to the top

Stern: The back of the boat

Tack: v. To turn a boat; n. the course a boat is following

Trim the sheet: To tighten the line that controls a sail, like the jib sheet

Turnbuckle: A device used to tighten a wire line

Uncleat: To remove a line from a cleat

V-berth: The forward double berth in the bow, so named because the point of the bow defines its shape

Wheel: The steering wheel of a sailboat

Wheel drum: A small circular device that accepts lines for turning

Wheelhouse: A place offering shelter and good visibility for the person steering a ship

Winches: Ratcheting devices for tightening lines that give great mechanical advantage

Windward mark: A buoy or race marker that lies in the general direction from which the wind is coming

About the Author

Jeff Jay is a writer living in Grosse Pointe Farms, Michigan. He's been messing around with boats since childhood, whether sailing, fishing, swimming, scuba diving, or cruising.

In his day job, Jeff works as an addictions counselor, and heads a national private practice of therapists. He has served as president of the Terry McGovern Foundation in Washington, D.C., and as trustee for several clinical and professional organizations. He currently sits on the advisory board of Jefferson House, part of the Capuchin ministries in Detroit, Michigan.

Jeff is a chronic daydreamer, brainstormer, and traveler. He is also a popular speaker on the subjects of spirituality and recovery. His previous books include the best-selling *Love First: A Family's Guide to Intervention* with Debra Jay. Learn more about his work at lovefirst.net.

About Hazelden Publishing

As part of the Hazelden Betty Ford Foundation, Hazelden Publishing offers both cutting-edge educational resources and inspirational books. Our print and digital works help guide individuals in treatment and recovery, and their loved ones. Professionals who work to prevent and treat addiction also turn to Hazelden Publishing for evidence-based curricula, digital content solutions, and videos for use in schools, treatment programs, correctional programs, and electronic health records systems. We also offer training for implementation of our curricula.

Through published and digital works, Hazelden Publishing extends the reach of healing and hope to individuals, families, and communities affected by addiction and related issues.

For more information about Hazelden publications, please call **800-328-9000** or visit us online at **hazelden.org/bookstore**.